Cambridge Eler

Elements in the Philosophy of
edited by
Yujin Nagasawa
University of Birmingham

GOD AND PRAYER

Scott A. Davison
Morehead State University

CAMBRIDGE
UNIVERSITY PRESS

CAMBRIDGE
UNIVERSITY PRESS

University Printing House, Cambridge CB2 8BS, United Kingdom

One Liberty Plaza, 20th Floor, New York, NY 10006, USA

477 Williamstown Road, Port Melbourne, VIC 3207, Australia

314–321, 3rd Floor, Plot 3, Splendor Forum, Jasola District Centre,
New Delhi – 110025, India

103 Penang Road, #05-06/07, Visioncrest Commercial, Singapore 238467

Cambridge University Press is part of the University of Cambridge.

It furthers the University's mission by disseminating knowledge in the pursuit of
education, learning, and research at the highest international levels of excellence.

www.cambridge.org
Information on this title: www.cambridge.org/9781108971430
DOI: 10.1017/9781108974967

First published 2022

A catalogue record for this publication is available from the British Library.

ISBN 978-1-108-97143-0 Paperback
ISSN 2399-5165 (online)
ISSN 2515-9763 (print)

God and Prayer

Elements in the Philosophy of Religion

DOI: 10.1017/9781108974967
First published online: February 2022

Scott A. Davison
Morehead State University

Author for correspondence: Scott A. Davison, s.davison@moreheadstate.edu

Abstract: Are there good reasons for offering petitionary prayers to God, if God exists? Could such prayers make a difference in the world? Could we ever have good reason to think that such prayers had been answered? In this Element, the author will carefully explore these questions with special attention to recent philosophical discussions.

Keywords: God, prayer, freedom, providence, religion

ISBNs: 9781108971430 (PB), 9781108974967 (OC)
ISSNs: 2399-5165 (online), 2515-9763 (print)

Contents

1 Introduction   1

2 Preliminary Considerations   2

3 Answered Petitionary Prayer   12

4 A Survey of Defenses   16

5 Epistemology   24

6 Practical Considerations and Quasi-Petitionary Prayer   34

7 Conclusion   42

References   43

1 Introduction

Not long ago, I was several hundred miles away from home, sitting on my sister's front porch. A hospice nurse just told me that my sister had only days left to live: the treatments that had served her well for the past few years had stopped working, and there was nothing medically left to do. (She would die two days later, as predicted.) I called my wife to tell her this terrible news and to ask her to join me right away. Before she could do that, she said, she needed to keep a medical appointment first.

My wife had completed extended treatments for breast cancer herself just a few years ago. She did not want to tell me that she had a medical appointment today because I was caring for my sister, but now she had to explain – the appointment was to investigate a new lump in her own breast.

My head started spinning with this news. For the next few hours, I would watch over my sister, work at my new job remotely, and wait for an update from my wife. Finally, she called to tell me that after two tests, the doctors concluded that there was nothing to worry about, and my sense of the world around me started to assume a more familiar shape.

While waiting to hear from my wife, I noticed that I felt drawn to pray for a good report for her, but I did not feel drawn to pray for my sister's recovery. What was the difference? If God could ensure that my wife did not have cancer again, why couldn't God heal my sister also? Does it make more sense to pray for things when it seems as if they might easily go one way or another but less sense to pray for them when the outcome seems determined or extremely unlikely? Why should anyone think that prayer could make a difference in terms of what God does in the first place?

These are some of the questions that have vexed philosophers over the centuries as they have thought carefully about petitionary prayer. In the pages that follow, I will explore the reasons people have offered for praying in the petitionary way, with special attention to recent philosophical work concerning these questions.

This recent work has tended to focus on three main questions. The first question is properly regarded as the classical problem of petitionary prayer: How can petitionary prayers make any difference to God? Very briefly, the worry is that petitionary prayers are either unnecessary (because God will do what is requested anyway because it is worth doing) or pointless (because God will not do what is requested because it is not worth doing). This question is addressed in Sections 3 and 4. The second question that is the focus of recent work concerning petitionary prayer involves epistemology: Could we ever know or reasonably believe that a given event was brought about by God as an answer to petitionary prayer? This question is addressed in Section 5. The third question is more practical: What should people request in petitionary prayer? This question is addressed in Section 6.

2 Preliminary Considerations

In this section, I discuss some important questions that frame the discussion of the remainder of this Element. They are general questions about God, prayer, and providence. People who are already quite familiar with the philosophical debate concerning petitionary prayer could easily skip this section, and so could people who are not interested in some of the subtleties of the debate. It provides a substantial framework for posing the key questions in a precise way, and I will refer to terminology and distinctions introduced in this section later in the Element. But if you find yourself losing interest in this section, please jump ahead to Section 3 and return to this section only if you feel the need to clarify something.

It turns out that there are many philosophical questions one could ask about prayer. It would be impossible to address all of them adequately in a single discussion, let alone a short one like this. To narrow the focus, I will discuss only prayer addressed to a divine being who is like the one worshiped by monotheists from the most prominent theistic religious traditions, including Judaism, Christianity, and Islam.

Most adherents of these religions believe that this God is absolutely perfect in power, knowledge, and goodness. But some philosophers and theologians have claimed that such a combination is impossible. I will not discuss those debates here. Instead, I will stipulate that when we talk about God, we mean a maximally excellent being who possesses the greatest possible combination of great-making qualities, whatever that turns out to be, and whether or not such a being actually exists.[1] I will refer to people who believe that such a God exists as *theists*.

I will not argue for or against the existence of God. For the sake of convenience, I will speak as if God exists, but questions about God and prayer are philosophically interesting whether or not this is true. None of my arguments will depend upon the assumption that God actually exists, and I will not assume that any particular religious practice or tradition has any advantage when it comes to understanding petitionary prayer philosophically.[2]

---

[1] See Nagasawa 2017 for a discussion of these debates, and a defense of this approach.

[2] As Caleb Cohoe has pointed out, though, different religious traditions might approach our central questions quite differently because they might rank the value of things in radically different ways; see the discussions of this question in Cohoe 2018 and a reply in Davison 2018.

There are many kinds of prayers that could be addressed to God. Some of them are designed to express beliefs and attitudes about God or God's actions, such as prayers of gratitude/thanks, adoration/praise, and lamentation/complaint. Others are designed to accomplish a change in one's relationship to God, such as prayers of confession or repentance. Finally, some prayers are designed to request something from God; I will call these petitionary prayers.[3] Although the other kinds of prayers raise interesting philosophical questions too, by far the most debate among philosophers arises in connection with petitionary prayers, so they will be the central focus of this Element.[4]

One of the main questions in the philosophical debate about petitionary prayer to date is whether there are good reasons for offering such prayers. Everyone admits that petitionary prayers make some difference, at least with respect to the person offering the prayer (for better or worse). For example, offering petitionary prayers might lead to peace of mind, or gratitude, or a welcome sense of dependence upon God; on the other hand, the belief that God's action in the world depends upon one's petitionary prayers could also lead to excessive guilt and reinforce irrational beliefs about the degree of one's control over the world.[5] But for philosophers of religion, the main question is usually whether petitionary prayers could make a difference to God's action in some sense. For example, are there things that God does in the world that God would not have done if petitionary prayers had not been offered for them?[6]

In offering petitionary prayers, people might request something from God that involves themselves, or another person or persons, or some other situation in the world. Such requests typically involve things in the future, but they can also involve things in the present or even in the past. In theory, petitionary prayers could even involve requests concerning eternal, necessary, or even impossible states of affairs – not even the sky is the limit, one might say.[7]

One way to frame the question about petitionary prayers making a difference to God involves the idea of God's reasons. Presumably, God has reasons for doing all sorts of things, some of them stronger than others. If there are things that are evil in themselves, for example, then presumably God has a conclusive

---

[3] This is not meant to be an exhaustive list of types of prayers; for more discussion, see Davison 2017, chapter 2.

[4] For more broad discussions of prayer in general, see Davison 2021b and 2021c.

[5] For more on possible effects, see the discussions in Phillips 1981, Murray and Meyers 1994, and Davison 2009.

[6] Here, I am bracketing off complicated issues about what it means for God to act in the world – philosophers of religion have a lot to say about this, but I cannot address those debates here. For a brief discussion of answered petitionary prayer and divine intervention, see Davison 2017, 14–16.

[7] For more complete classification of types of petitionary prayers, see Davison 2017, chapter 2.

reason not to do them – God's moral perfection is incompatible with granting requests that would involve God doing anything that is evil in itself.

There may also be connections between things that God has conclusive reasons not to break or connections between things that not even God can break. For instance, theists have typically thought that God has a providential plan for the world that is contingent, where this implies that God could have chosen a different one instead. There may also be things that are literally beyond God's control. For example, theists have typically held that no matter how earnestly a person prays for God to make it false that $2 + 2 = 4$, there is nothing God can do about that – it's a logical truth that could not be otherwise. Most theists have also thought that God cannot change the past – once something has happened, they would say, it cannot be undone.[8]

If we put together all of God's reasons for making the world a certain way, is there any room left for petitionary prayers to make a difference in how things go? This is one way of framing the main question that has dominated contemporary philosophical debates about reasons for offering petitionary prayers. As I will use the term here, a *challenge* to petitionary prayer is an argument designed to show that the answer to this question is "no," to explain why petitionary prayers cannot make a difference to God in some relevant sense. By contrast, a *defense* of petitionary prayer is designed to provide a possible explanation of how petitionary prayer might make a difference to God in some relevant sense.[9]

We can imagine different standards for success for challenges and defenses, respectively.[10] Depending on what people think is at stake, they might have higher or lower standards for success. For example, a deeply skeptical nontheist might find the possible existence of God unwelcome in various ways[11] and so might demand very strong evidence for the possibility that petitionary prayers could be answered by God before even considering apparent cases of answered petitionary prayer. For such a person, a defense is not likely to be successful unless it explains clearly why God might make the provision of certain things dependent upon the offering of petitionary prayer over a wide range of realistic cases.

---

[8] See the discussion of this in Adams and Kretzmann 1983. However, it may be possible for God to bring about something that is a response to a future petitionary prayer; for more on this, see Flint 1998, chapter 11, Timpe 2005, and Mawson 2007.

[9] For a slightly different use of these terms, and a more complete discussion of examples of both challenges and defenses, see Davison 2017, 16–23.

[10] Thanks to Scott Hill, Caleb Cohoe, and Daniel Howard-Snyder for suggesting the brief discussion of this question that follows.

[11] For a helpful collection of essays exploring the question of whether we should want God to exist or not, see Kraay 2020.

By contrast, a highly confident theist mind finds it unwelcome to consider the possibility that God does not or cannot answer petitionary prayers and so might demand very strong evidence for that conclusion. For such a person, a challenge is not likely to be successful unless it explains clearly why God would not (or could not) make the provision of certain things dependent upon the offering of petitionary prayers in clearly possible cases.

With respect to challenges, typically philosophers try to show that no petitionary prayers of any kind could or would be answered by God for various reasons. This is a very wide and sweeping conclusion. By contrast, with respect to defenses, typically philosophers try to show only that God has good reasons for making the provision of certain things dependent upon the offering of petitionary prayers in just some cases. In this respect, anyway, philosophers trying to provide a defense are engaged in an easier task than those trying to provide a challenge, all other things being equal. However, it makes sense to count a defense of petitionary prayer as *fully* successful only if it provides an explanation that makes sense of the full range of cases in which theists typically hold that petitionary prayers are appropriate. These include cases of petitionary prayer for one's own self or others, for the provision of some good thing or the prevention/removal of some bad thing, whether it be physical or spiritual, trivial or serious, and so on.

Given the wide range of possible criteria for success for defenses and challenges mentioned, it is difficult to speak in general terms about whether the arguments developed by philosophers with respect to petitionary prayer are successful. In the discussion that follows, out of necessity, I will typically ignore these differences for the sake of brevity. So when asking whether a defense is successful, I will be asking whether strong evidence has been provided for the conclusion that it would be reasonable for God to make the provision of things dependent upon the offering of petitionary prayers across the full range of cases in which theists typically believe that petitionary prayers should be offered. Of course, it is not easy to determine what counts as a good reason for God here – in part, that is why these questions are philosophical ones. Partial defenses are better than nothing, and perhaps it is possible to combine them; I will return to that question in Section 5.

By contrast, when asking whether a challenge is successful, I will be asking whether strong evidence has been provided for thinking that God could not or would not make the provision of anything dependent upon the offering of petitionary prayers. I will discuss some challenges in this section and then turn to defenses in Section 3. Typically, challenges to petitionary prayer appeal to God's goodness or God's knowledge. For instance, sometimes people argue that because God is perfectly good, God will provide what is best for everyone, all the time, whether or not petitionary prayers are offered.[12] Such arguments sometimes generate questions similar to those that arise in connection with philosophical discussions of the problem of evil: Why does God permit bad things to happen in the world in the first place?

Here I think it is helpful to distinguish questions about the problem of evil in general from questions about why God might require petitionary prayers before providing certain things. Here is one way to explain the difference. Suppose that a certain person, Pat, has fallen ill. Without knowing anything more about the situation, we can distinguish several different possibilities concerning how petitionary prayers on Pat's behalf might relate to God's reasons for healing Pat:

(1) For reasons that are independent of any petitionary prayers, God will heal Pat and would have done so whether or not any petitionary prayers were offered on Pat's behalf. (If this is the case, then petitionary prayer would make no difference with respect to Pat's healing.)

(2) God will heal Pat if petitionary prayers are offered on Pat's behalf by certain persons in certain circumstances, but not otherwise. (If this is the case, petitionary prayer would make all the difference for Pat's healing.)

(3) For reasons that are completely independent of any petitionary prayers, God will not heal Pat and would not have done so whether or not any petitionary prayers were offered on Pat's behalf. (If this is the case, then petitionary prayer would make no difference with respect to Pat's healing.)

There may be other possibilities here, too – I am not claiming that these are the only three. But we can identify at least these three. I am not suggesting that one of these three options holds in *every* case of illness – I am just saying that with respect to *Pat's* illness specifically, we can distinguish these three possibilities from the outset, and they clearly differ with respect to the difference that petitionary prayer would make.

Returning to the question raised earlier, we were trying to explain the difference between questions about the problem of evil in general and questions about why God might require petitionary prayers before providing certain things. With respect to these three possibilities involving Pat's illness, those who take up the problem of evil in general are trying to identify what God's reasons might be in cases like (3), where God has reasons for not healing Pat that God clearly lacks in cases like (1). By contrast, those who offer defenses of petitionary prayer are trying to identify what God's reasons might be in cases like (2). So

---

[12] For an example of an argument developed along these lines (roughly speaking), see Basinger 1983; for a more complete list of challenges to petitionary prayer from the history of philosophy, see Davison 2017, 16–21.

although these two questions are related to one another in interesting ways, and people often discuss them as if they are the same, they are logically distinct.[13]

In response to the challenge that petitionary prayer is pointless because God will provide what is best whether or not petitionary prayers are offered, some philosophers have argued that there are compelling reasons for God to make the provision of certain things dependent upon the offering of petitionary prayers; in a way, these possible explanations of God's reasons make up the bulk of the philosophical literature concerning petitionary prayer. I will discuss and evaluate most of these proposed defenses in some detail in Section 3.

At this point, it seems important to recognize that debates about petitionary prayer are logically independent of debates about whether or not human beings have freedom of choice. Although some defenses of petitionary prayer assume that created persons offer their petitionary prayers freely in some libertarian sense, which requires that they not be determined in what they do by factors beyond their control, not all defenses have this feature. Heath White, for instance, embraces Theological Determinism, which implies that humans never make free choices in any libertarian sense. But he argues that petitionary prayers sometimes make all the difference in terms of what God does in the world.[14] This example illustrates a fascinating fact about philosophical debates concerning petitionary prayer: different people find it important to preserve very different things in their understanding of how petitionary prayer might make a difference to God.

Returning again to the question of challenges to petitionary prayer, another common kind of challenge appeals to the extent of God's knowledge of the future. This challenge involves arguing that petitionary prayers cannot make any difference in terms of what God does because God already knows the future, so there is no point in praying about it – either what you might request is already part of the future, or it is not, and either way, the prayer will make no difference. In order to explore this kind of challenge in some detail, it is necessary to discuss the main ways in which people understand God's knowledge of the future and how this relates to God's providential control over the world. Although I cannot describe adequately the complex debate over these views here, at least I can provide a summary of the main issues that philosophers debate in this area.

---

[13] For additional discussion concerning the relationship between unanswered petitionary prayers and the problem of evil, see Taliaferro 2007, Veber 2007, Franks 2009, Davison 2017, chapter 6, and Mooney and Grafton-Cardwell (under review).

[14] According to White, our prayers are final causes, not efficient causes, of divine action; see White 2019, 33–6. Here White is appealing to a taxonomy of causes that can be traced back to Aristotle; for more on this causal framework, see Falcon 2019.

According to the view called Open Theism, some things about the future are not determined yet, so not even God can know about them at the present time.[15] Since they are libertarians about free will, which implies that they understand such choices to be not fully determined by prior conditions beyond an agent's control, Open Theists hold that these unknowable things include the future free choices of human beings. For example, the ancient philosopher Aristotle seems to have held that it is indeterminate today whether or not there will be a sea battle tomorrow – so many ships will pass by each other, and so many individual people will be making decisions based upon whom they encounter, that it is literally up in the air today whether or not a battle will break out tomorrow on the sea.[16] That part of the future is open, we might say – things could go either way.

Open Theists note that God still knows everything that can be known, including all possibilities and probabilities concerning the future, so God has the most complete knowledge of the future possible. But they insist that God does not know exactly what human beings will freely do in the future. If our future petitionary prayers are free, or God's decision whether to answer such prayers is free (or both), then those things are undetermined until they happen, so petitionary prayer can make all the difference in the world – God's knowledge of the future does not threaten petitionary prayer at all, and the challenge can be answered easily.

Although Open Theism has become more popular than ever during the past thirty years or so, some people find it to be unacceptable as an account of divine providence. One reason often discussed in this connection is that since Open Theism denies that God knows the future in all of its detail, it suggests that God takes risks in creation, and some people find this idea objectionable.[17]

A very different approach to divine providence seems to avoid this objection, although it certainly has issues of its own. This second view is called the Middle Knowledge account.[18] According to this approach, God knows the complete future in all of its detail as a result of inferring it logically from two other things: (1) exactly what would happen in any possible situation and (2) which situations will actually arise.[19] For example, according to the Middle Knowledge view, God would know what each sailor would do in every circumstance, and God would know exactly which circumstances would arise tomorrow on the sea.

---

[15] See Hasker 1989, Rissler 2006, and Borland 2017.

[16] For a lively discussion of Aristotle's reasoning here, see Anscombe 1956.

[17] I am not suggesting that this is a decisive objection to Open Theism, of course; for more on the debate here, see Hasker 1989, Flint 1998, Borland 2017, and Rissler 2017.

[18] This approach is sometimes called "Molinism," after the sixteenth-century theologian Luis de Molina, who appears to have first clearly articulated this position.

[19] See Flint 1998 and Molina 2004.

Based on this knowledge, God will be able to infer logically what each sailor will choose to do, even if those choices are free in some libertarian sense, so God will know today whether or not there will be a sea battle tomorrow. According to this view, even though God knows exactly what you will do in the future, it will still be up to you to decide what to do then – in fact, when you act freely, you have the ability to do something such that, if you were to do it, God would have always known something different about the future.[20]

According to the Middle Knowledge approach, petitionary prayer can make all the difference because God knows prior to creating the world which prayers would be offered freely by which persons in which circumstances, so God can take this information into account from eternity when deciding what to create. The Middle Knowledge approach also helps to explain why God would decide not to answer certain petitionary prayers because God would also know what would happen if they were answered – and sometimes this might be very bad.[21]

Although the Middle Knowledge view is certainly a key player in the debate about divine providence, appearing to permit theists to have their cake and eat it too (by combining a robust picture of human freedom with a strong sense of divine control), some people find it unacceptable. One reason is that people doubt whether there are truths about what everyone and everything would do in every situation, and if there are, they wonder whether anyone (even God) could know them.[22]

By contrast, the Timeless Eternity approach to divine knowledge appeals to the idea that God is outside of time altogether and sees all of history simultaneously from the perspective of eternity. According to this view, God does not really know *in advance* what will happen in the future because God is not located anywhere in time. To use an analogy from St. Thomas Aquinas (1225–74 CE), imagine travelers moving through a valley in the middle of a line of wagons. They can see the wagon in front and the wagon behind, but nothing else. This is a limited view that corresponds to the perspective of persons in time. But now imagine someone on top of a nearby hill who can see the entire line of wagons at once. This all-encompassing view corresponds to the view of God from outside of time, who sees all of history at once from the point of view of eternity.[23]

---

[20] This point is made in Flint 1998 – the most detailed and clearly articulated presentation of the Middle Knowledge view in the literature.

[21] See the discussion of this possibility, with respect to Cuthbert and an iguana, in Flint 1998, chapter 10; also see the discussion of praying for things to have occurred in the past in Flint 1998, chapter 11.

[22] See Hasker 1989, Davison 1991, Flint 1998, Zagzebski 2017, Borland 2017, and Rissler 2017.

[23] See Deng 2018.

The Timeless Eternity approach seems to have trouble with this challenge to petitionary prayer based upon divine knowledge of the future – if God sees from eternity what petitionary prayers people offer, God must also see from eternity everything else about the world, including what God does. It is hard to understand the idea of God responding to requests from the point of view of eternity because that idea seems to involve holding fixed the requests and then God choosing some response without already knowing what the response would be.

The problem here seems very similar to the problem that attaches to a different view of God's knowledge that is often called the Simple Foreknowledge view. According to the Simple Foreknowledge view, God is not outside of time but foreknows the future in all of its detail, including those parts of the future that are not determined by past events, such as human free choices (understood in some libertarian sense). As a number of authors have pointed out, God's knowledge of the future comes too late to make a difference – after all, the future is whatever will actually happen, not what might happen or could happen. Since God knows only what is actually going to be future on the Simple Foreknowledge view, and not what would have happened if things had been different, God cannot change the future in response to what God knows about it, and so cannot respond to petitionary prayers on the basis of simple foreknowledge about the future.[24]

There is one more view of providence to consider here. It is called Theological Determinism. According to this approach, God knows the past, present, and future because God decides exactly how things will be, by determining them in every detail.[25] Because God completely determines that people will offer various petitionary prayers at various times, God can also decide whether and how to answer them. People tend to object to Theological Determinism in many of the same ways that they object to other kinds of determinism, by asking how it makes sense to attribute moral responsibility to created agents if God exercises complete control over creation; they also wonder whether Theological Determinism generates an insoluble version of the problem of evil that undercuts the claim that God is morally perfect.[26]

---

[24] This argument is a matter of some controversy; see the discussions of this question in Hasker 1989 and Flint 1998, along with more recent debates in Pruss 2007, Hasker 2009, and Hunt 2009.

[25] Theological Determinism is neutral on the question of whether God is outside of time; for more on this view of providence, see Furlong 2019 and White 2019.

[26] For further discussion, see Frankfurt 1969, Van Inwagen 1983, Dennett 1984, Wolf 1990, Fischer and Ravizza 1998, Kane 1998, Pereboom 2001, 2014, Watson 2003, Timpe 2013, Timpe and Speak 2016, and Ekstrom 2021. For additional discussions focused on the nature of divine freedom, see Van Inwagen 1983, 2006, Wierenga 2002, Mawson 2005, Bergmann and Cover 2006, Talbott 2009, Timpe 2013, and White 2019.

Except for Timeless Eternity and Simple Foreknowledge, then, each of these approaches to the nature of divine providence permits at least the possibility of petitionary prayers making a difference in God's action, so they each provide the resources to answer the challenge to petitionary prayer based on an appeal to the extent of God's knowledge of the future. These different approaches to divine providence also have different implications for what might count as an answer to petitionary prayer. Must answered prayer involve a miracle, for instance? In order to avoid taking any specific stand concerning the nature of miracles, for the purposes of our brief discussion here, let's just say that a miracle is an event that is not part of the natural course of things.[27]

According to Open Theism, if someone offers a petitionary prayer freely (in some libertarian sense of "freely"), then God would not have known in advance that it would be offered (although God would have known the probability that this would happen). This means that God could not have arranged the world in advance as a response to the future petitionary prayer, in order to ensure that the thing requested would occur as part of the natural course of events. So, if the thing requested was not part of the natural course of events and God brings it about in response to petitionary prayer, then it looks like a miracle.

On the other hand, if the thing requested in petitionary prayer is part of the natural course of events, then it need not be a miracle from the point of view of Open Theism. Would such a thing constitute a mere coincidence, though, and not an answer to petitionary prayer? One way to approach this question would be to consider whether God would have brought about the thing requested, at least in part because it was requested, had it not been part of the natural course of events. If the answer here is "yes," then maybe the proponent of Open Theism could argue that this should count as a case of answered petitionary prayer. But if the answer here is "no," then it seems like a coincidence that the thing requested occurred after the petitionary prayer was offered, in which case it would not count as a case of answered prayer. So maybe the Open Theist need not say that all answered prayers involve miracles.

By contrast, the proponents of both Middle Knowledge and Theological Determinism can claim that God could arrange the natural course of events in advance so that it included things that God knew would be requested in future petitionary prayers. From the Middle Knowledge point of view, God would know through Middle Knowledge what all persons would freely do in all situations in which they could be placed. This means that God would know which petitionary prayers would be offered and could then adjust the future

---

[27] Here, I am avoiding yet another substantial philosophical debate; for more information, see Nagasawa 2018 and McGrew 2019.

from eternity, so to speak, in order to answer them. From the perspective of Theological Determinism, God would know from eternity which petitionary prayers would be determined to be offered because God would have decided this, and God could also decide which ones would be answered. So those who subscribe to Middle Knowledge or Theological Determinism are not committed to the claim that all answered prayers require miracles, either.

This completes my general discussion of larger questions about God, prayer, providence, and challenges. At this point, I will turn to questions about what it means to say that God has answered a petitionary prayer, along with defenses designed to explain how and why God might do so, with special attention to recent work concerning these questions.

3 Answered Petitionary Prayer

For some people, it seems important to be able to say whether petitionary prayers have definitely been answered in actual or hypothetical cases. For example, this could be because they believe that answered petitionary prayers provide some evidence for God's existence or providential concern or because they play some important role in one's relationship with God. For others, it might be important to say whether petitionary prayers have definitely been answered because they are skeptics about petitionary prayer and they want to collect evidence to support their skepticism. In this section, I will investigate in some detail what it means to say that a petitionary prayer has been answered. Some people are surprised to discover that this turns out to be a rather complicated question all by itself. Without exploring every facet of this question, I will explain why it is a complicated one and then provide a framework for classifying the different approaches that people have taken to this question.

What do we mean when we say that God answered a petitionary prayer? Just because I ask God to bring about some event and that event happens, it does not follow immediately that God has answered my prayer – there must be some connection between these two things, and it cannot just be a coincidence that they happened together.[28] There is also the question of whether God answers a petitionary prayer when God addresses the underlying intention behind it, even if God does not provide exactly what was requested.[29]

Some petitionary prayers seem not to be answered in any sense – not only does the specific state of affairs requested never come to be, but the intentions behind the requesting of that state of affairs are also not addressed. For those

---

[28] For more on this question, see the discussion in Davison 2017, chapter 2.

[29] See the helpful discussion of this point in Finley 2019, 393–4, to be discussed in more detail in Sections 4 and 5.

who claim that God answers all petitionary prayers, this seems to be a problem. In response to this problem, some philosophers distinguish two related things: There are answered petitionary prayers, on the one hand, and there are replies to petitionary prayers, on the other hand.[30] Not every reply to a petitionary prayer constitutes an answered petitionary prayer, according to this approach; sometimes, God might reply "no" to a petitionary prayer, for good reasons.[31] According to this approach, although God does not answer every petitionary prayer, God replies to every petitionary prayer.

Recently, Daniel Johnson has drawn attention to an interesting feature of explanation in general that sheds new light on the debate about what it means to say that a petitionary prayer has been answered. He observes that when we try to understand why something has happened, what we count as a successful explanation depends, in part, on our interests. Although there might be a complete, interest-independent explanation for something, this is almost never available to us, and typically, it is not interesting to us (Johnson 2020, 142). Instead, "The context and the inquirer's interests allow certain partial and non-ultimate explanations to stand in as a satisfactory answer to the 'why' question, while disallowing others" (Johnson 2020, 142).

In his approach to questions about answered prayers, Johnson follows Alexander Pruss in thinking that God is omnirational, where this means that God performs every action on the basis of "all and only those reasons that are unexcluded (good) reasons for that action" (Pruss 2013, 4). By an "unexcluded" reason, Pruss means a reason that has not been excluded by some higher-order reason, such as an authoritative command or a valid promise.[32] According to Pruss, it is relatively easy to answer (affirmatively) when we ask whether our petitionary prayers have been answered, at least when that which we requested was good and it comes to be. Here is why:

> A request for a good always provides the requestee with a reason to provide the good, at least barring some exclusionary reason . . .. Therefore, if a good is requested from God, and God provides the good, then unless the request-based reason was excluded, the good was provided at least in part because it was requested. So all we need to know is that x prayed for a good and x obtained the good to know that the good came *at least* in part due to prayer.
> (Pruss 2013, 16–17, italics in the original)

Elsewhere, I have argued that Pruss's approach provides an unsatisfactory account of what it means for God to answer a prayer. This is because his

---

[30] For example, see Davison 2017, chapter 2. [31] See Flint 1998, 222–7, for example.
[32] For human beings, these qualifications would exclude personal preferences from figuring into rational deliberations: see Pruss 2013, 2–3.

approach implies that we should count God as having answered petitionary prayers even in cases where God has independent, conclusive reasons to bring about that which was requested anyway so that God would have done the same thing even if no prayer had been offered at all.[33]

By way of reply to my critique of Pruss, Johnson questions my assumption that in order for prayers to be answered by God, they must make a difference in this specific sense. His argument is helpful and informative:

> Perhaps it is enough that our requests make *a* difference in the sense that they are one of God's reasons for acting, even if they don't make *the* difference in the sense of constituting a tipping point that takes God from not acting to acting. And omnirationality entails that it is easy for our requests to make a difference in that way, because so long as the request actually gives God *a* reason to act, he acts at least in part on the basis of that request.
>
> (Johnson 2020, 138, italics in the original)

Johnson makes an important point here, whether or not we agree with his assumption that God is omnirational in Pruss's sense. People have different reasons for caring about why God has answered their prayers, and this makes a difference to them in terms of what counts as God's having answered them. Johnson illustrates this with a number of helpful examples; in one of them, he imagines being paralyzed and stuck in a house and still wanting to be part of what God is doing. He says that:

> If that is my interest, then what matters is not whether my prayer "made the difference;" what matters is that God took what I asked him into account, that I got to be "part of the team," even if God didn't need me on the team.
>
> (Johnson 2020, 145)

Johnson also mentions similar cases in which people are content to play a certain role even if their participation might not make a difference in some strong sense.[34] These include cases in which people advocate for political change, play a tiny role in some large-scale rescue effort, or participate in team sports (Johnson 2020, 146). Johnson claims that his approach to questions about answered prayer also has another theoretical benefit: it helps make sense of cases of praying for things that God has already promised to bring about (Johnson 2020, 146).[35]

---

[33] See Davison 2017, 34–7; for an insightful discussion of omnirationality and divine freedom, see Rice 2016.

[34] In private correspondence, Daniel and Frances Howard-Snyder have wondered whether these kinds of prayers satisfy the conditions for speech acts to count as petitions at all; for further discussion of those conditions, see Howard-Snyder and Howard-Snyder 2010.

[35] For another approach to this question, see the discussion of the Lord's Prayer in Stump 1979, the landmark article that started the contemporary debate about petitionary prayer.

Johnson agrees that in addition to the contexts mentioned previously, in which people just want to play some role, however small, there are also contexts in which people care about whether petitionary prayers made *the* difference to God's action in some strong way. For example, perhaps our goal in offering petitionary prayers is actually to change God's mind or to be partly responsible for some changes in the world or to be in friendship with God in a way that involves our autonomy (Johnson 2020, 152–3). In those situations, we might insist that our prayers are answered only if they make a relevant difference to what God does.

Johnson's point about the different interests that people have in asking whether or not their prayers have been answered suggests two general families of approaches to our question about answered petitionary prayers: some approaches insist that petitionary prayers make *the* difference with respect to God's action in the world in some strong sense in order to be classified as answered, whereas other approaches do not insist upon this. I will call the former *difference-making* approaches and the latter *non-difference-making* approaches.

According to a difference-making approach to the question of answered petitionary prayer, as I have defined it here, we should count a prayer as answered by God only if it makes a difference to God's action in the world in some strong sense. In trying to specify this condition precisely, it is tempting to require something like counterfactual dependence between the offering of the petitionary prayer and God's action, as many authors have done. This would involve saying that God answers a petitionary prayer by doing something only if God would not have done the same thing if the prayer had not been offered. But even though this makes sense in many cases, it does not always seem to be necessary.[36] Rather than try to answer this question once and for all, we should probably permit each difference-making approach to explain for itself what counts as making a difference.

However, all difference-making approaches do share an interesting pattern. To see the pattern, notice first that if the thing requested by petitionary prayers is really, really good, then God might have conclusive reasons for bringing it about anyway, even if nobody ever offered any petitionary prayers for it. But given the way difference-making approaches understand answered prayer, such cases would not constitute examples of answered prayer because the prayers in question would not have made any difference to God (see Davison 2017, 34). So, for difference-making approaches, the offering of a petitionary prayer must make a difference to God, in some strong sense – it must add value to the

---

[36] See the discussion of the literature in Davison 2017, 27–8.

situation in some way. As Michael Murray and Kurt Meyers say, a successful (difference-making) defense of petitionary prayer must identify "some good which accrues as a result of the petition being made, a good significant enough to be worth foregoing the (lesser) good of the provision being made without the request."[37] I will call this the *value-adding constraint* for difference-making defenses of petitionary prayer.

Here is an example designed to illustrate this constraint. If I pray for the healing of a mother of five children who is suffering from terminal cancer and God heals her in response to my prayer, then the difference-making approach is committed to something like the claim that God would not have healed her had I not prayed.[38] This means they must say that healing her when no prayers had been offered for this would not be as good as healing her in response to petitionary prayer. What good does God obtain by making the provision of some things dependent (in some way) upon the offering of petitionary prayers? Difference-making defenses provide different ways of satisfying the value-adding constraint, with varying degrees of success. In the following section, we will consider several different approaches.

This completes my exploration of the question of what it means to say that God has answered a petitionary prayer. Some additional complications will come up later, but the distinction between difference-making and non-difference-making approaches should help us navigate the different accounts people have proposed to explain why petitionary prayers are important with respect to God.

4 A Survey of Defenses

In this section, I will provide a survey of defenses of petitionary prayer. In the end, I will argue that although each kind of defense has some merit, no single defense seems to explain, all by itself, why people might find it reasonable to offer petitionary prayers across the full range of ordinary circumstances in which people commonly hold that such prayers would be appropriate. But as we will see later, this might not be a very significant result, in terms of the total reasons people have to offer petitionary prayers.

Some defenses of petitionary prayer argue that God makes the provision of things dependent upon the offering of petitionary prayers in order to extend and enhance *human responsibility* for the character of the world. For these defenses, the additional human responsibility satisfies the value-adding constraint described previously. As Richard Swinburne says, "If human responsibility is

---

[37] Murray and Meyers 1994, 313; see also the discussion of related points in Veber 2007 and Pickup 2018.

[38] See Davison 2017, 75.

good, then this extension to it – of exerting influence on (though not of course compelling) God to change things [through petitionary prayer] – would surely also be good" (Swinburne 1998, 115). I will call these *responsibility-based defenses*.

There are different ways in which one might develop a complete responsibility-based defense. One might ask, for instance, whether the responsibility involved is intrinsically or instrumentally valuable (or both) and whether there is an optimal level of such responsibility. But all versions would agree that the added responsibility generated by making the provision of certain things dependent upon the offering of petitionary prayers explains God's decision to create this arrangement.[39]

Responsibility-based defenses are clear examples of what we have called difference-making approaches because they typically involve the claim that if petitionary prayers are not offered for certain things, then God will not bring them about, even if there are really significant consequences.[40] Because of the difference-making connection between asking and receiving, advocates for responsibility-based defenses argue that if God did not make the provision of certain things dependent upon the offering of petitionary prayers, human beings would not have as much responsibility for the world as they do.

Ever since philosophers started asking about the conditions necessary for responsibility in general, some have argued that people must have some choice in order to be properly held responsible – if they have no choice at all and what they do is inevitable, then they cannot be responsible for anything.[41] Many who advocate responsibility-based defenses of petitionary prayer embrace the idea that having an independent choice is necessary for responsibility, so they hold that human beings possess some kind of libertarian freedom (at least with respect to their petitionary prayers). But one need not embrace that claim in order to argue that petitionary prayer makes a difference to God. As noted previously, for instance, Heath White endorses Theological Determinism but also argues that requests to God sometimes make all the difference in terms of God's action (see White 2019, 33–6). So advocates of responsibility-based defenses need not embrace libertarianism about human freedom, as long as they can make sense of responsibility without it.[42]

---

[39] For a more detailed discussion of some prominent responsibility-based defenses, see Davison 2017, chapter 7.

[40] According to the discussion in Howard-Snyder and Howard-Snyder 2010, this is the "Puzzle of Serious Petitionary Prayer" (Howard-Snyder and Howard-Snyder 2010, 64–6).

[41] The earliest systematic discussion of this question is probably found in Aristotle 2014, book III, chapters 1–5.

[42] For a more detailed discussion of some of the alternative possibilities here, see Davison 2017, chapter 7.

Some who advance responsibility-based defenses claim that the offering of petitionary prayers is necessary and sufficient, in the circumstances, for the outcome that God brings about in response to those prayers.[43] This claim raises interesting questions about divine freedom because typically we imagine that God is free either to answer a given petitionary prayer or not. If God is free not to answer a given petitionary prayer, it would seem not to be true that the offering of the petitionary prayer is sufficient for the outcome that God brings about in response.[44]

In general, though, being responsible for some outcome does not require that if one had failed to act, then the outcome in question would not have occurred. This is one clear lesson to be drawn from the controversy concerning the so-called principle of alternative possibilities.[45] To illustrate why, notice that more than one person can bring about a single state of affairs. Suppose I decide to take out the trash, but had I not done this, you would have done so instead. This means that the trash would have been taken out even if I did not do it myself. But that does not imply that I have no responsibility for the trash being taken out – I may be fully responsible for this, even though it would have happened anyway.

Since God is the one answering petitionary prayers, it might be tempting to argue that God should get all of the responsibility for answered prayers, and the human petitioner should get none of it. But it is worth noting that the presence of intervening agents does not automatically diminish responsibility.[46] It is also important to note that it is possible for more than one agent to be fully responsible for a single outcome.[47] So advocates of responsibility-based defenses have plausible responses to concerns about intervening agents and shared responsibility.

A number of other objections have been raised against responsibility-based defenses of petitionary prayer. Some have wondered whether the degree of responsibility involved here could be very significant, whether it is always good to extend responsibility in general and whether considerations of luck undermine the importance of responsibility. Most importantly, it is not clear that the extra responsibility added to the world through God's decision to require petitionary prayers in some cases is important enough to justify God in

---

[43] For example, Howard-Snyder and Howard-Snyder 2010, 59–60.

[44] For more detailed discussions of divine freedom and petitionary prayer, see Davison 2017, chapter 3, 2021c; for a discussion of the relationship between pride and answered prayer, see Davison 2022.

[45] See the landmark discussion in Frankfurt 1969, along with a further diagnosis of the literature in Fischer and Ravizza 1998.

[46] See Zimmerman 1985b and the critical discussions of Davison 2009 in Howard-Snyder and Howard-Snyder 2010 and Choi 2016.

[47] For a defense of this claim, see Zimmerman 1985a.

withholding significant goods that could have been provided, especially for third parties.[48] But there seems to be no way to rule out the possibility that there are cases in which the main lines of the responsibility-based defense are correct: perhaps sometimes God really does answer petitionary prayers because it extends human responsibility for the character of the world. In terms of what counts as a successful defense, the responsibility-based approach seems to be at least partly successful.

Turning now to other kinds of defense, Thomas P. Flint argues that the offering of petitionary prayer can change the circumstances in which God acts. The example he offers to illustrate this idea comes from the Christian scriptures and involves various ways in which a public prayer brings possible outcomes into play that otherwise would not be available to God. In the example, Peter approaches a man who was known to be unable to walk from birth and says, "In the name of Jesus Christ of Nazareth, rise and walk!" (Acts chapter 3). Flint claims that an implicit prayer to God to heal this man changes the circumstances in such a way that God now has a number of reasons to heal the lame man that would not have been present had the prayer not been offered (see Flint 1998, 222–7). Although it is not clear to me that petitionary prayer per se is doing the work in these kinds of cases,[49] the idea that petitionary prayers change (or bring about) the circumstances in which God acts has wide appeal.

For instance, the idea that all by themselves, requests provide new reasons for God to act is very popular in the literature; it is the basis of what I will call *request-based defenses*. Appealing to the work of Geoffrey Cupit (1994), Daniel and Frances Howard-Snyder argue that when people request good things from God, those requests provide God with new, additional reasons to bring those things about (Howard-Snyder and Howard-Snyder 2010). Although it is not clear whether the specific account Cupit provides can apply in a straightforward way to requests made to God,[50] others have also advanced similar claims.[51]

Request-based defenses attempt to address the value-adding constraint for difference-making approaches to petitionary prayer by claiming that human requests by themselves make a difference in terms of the values at stake in a given situation. God might have lots of reasons for bringing about something, but when we ask for it, that provides an additional reason for doing so – and

---

[48] See the discussions in Howard-Snyder and Howard-Snyder 2010 and Davison 2017, chapter 7.
[49] See the discussion in Davison 2017, 28–33.
[50] For more on this question, see the critical discussion in Davison 2017, 101–4, and the discussion of the relevance of the value of the request in Thornton (under review).
[51] Including Alexander Pruss (2013), Caleb Cohoe (2014), and Gianluca Di Muzio (2018).

sometimes that additional reason might make all the difference. For instance, according to Ryan Mattew Parker and Bradley Rettler, our requests in petitionary prayer sometimes serve as something like a tiebreaker for God: "When the [possible] worlds are tied, he has to just pick one. And our prayers influence which one he picks" (Parker and Rettler 2017, 185).

In some cases, it seems clear that it is better to give something in response to a request, rather than giving the same thing unsolicited. But in the case of really serious needs, that explanation seems to become somewhat strained – we sometimes think it is better to help others even if they do not (or cannot) request it.[52] So it is not clear that request-based defenses can address the value-adding constraint in a way that is satisfying for every kind of situation in which people typically think that petitionary prayers are appropriate. But perhaps they explain why God would be justified in providing certain things only if they are requested, at least in some cases. To that extent, they would be successful defenses.

Sometimes, people argue that God would make the provision of certain good things dependent upon petitionary prayers not because of the value added by the request per se but because of the effects of such an arrangement upon one's relationship with God. As I will describe them here, *relationship-based defenses* articulate some good that arises in relationship with God that requires a difference-making arrangement involving petitionary prayers. For instance, in her classic paper on petitionary prayer, which launched the current debate among philosophers working in the analytic tradition, Eleonore Stump argues that petitionary prayer is needed for the possibility of a friendship with God that is free from overwhelming spoiling and overwhelming oppression (Stump 1979; see also Embry 2018, 136–7). Michael Murray and Kurt Meyers also argue that God's requiring petitionary prayers before providing certain goods helps increase our gratitude and teach us things about God's purpose and nature (Murray and Meyers 1994).

In a related vein, Charles Taliaferro argues that petitionary prayer permits the existence of what he calls a "mediatory good," where this involves "the valuable mediation of a good agent" (Taliaferro 2007, 621–2). Nicholas Smith and Thomas Yip argue that without God's answering petitionary prayers, we could not have real partnership with God (Smith and Yip 2010). Vincent Brümmer argues that the two-way contingency required for real personal relationships implies that our petitionary prayers must make a difference in relation to God, and this contingency prevents depersonalization of our

---

[52] Questions about autonomy and paternalism are relevant here; see the discussion in Davison 2017, chapter 7.

connection to God (Brümmer 2008). And Caleb Cohoe and Isaac Choi also appeal to the value of petitionary prayer in enhancing friendship with God (Cohoe 2014, 40, Choi 2016, 43).

Speaking very generally, relationship-based defenses attempt to satisfy the value-adding constraint for difference-making approaches to petitionary prayer by claiming that there is a certain kind of goodness involved in relationship with God that requires an arrangement that involves petitionary prayer as a necessary ingredient. Historically, many theists have thought that being in relationship with God is the highest possible good for human beings, so this approach often resonates with those who are inclined in that direction. Not every way of defending the connection here is equally plausible,[53] but I think we should agree that in some cases at least, relationship-based defenses do explain why God might require petitionary prayers before providing some good things, at least on some occasions. This makes the defense at least partially successful.[54]

All of the defenses I have considered so far in this section have argued that God requires petitionary prayers before providing certain good things because this arrangement leads to the production of good things (distinct from the object requested in the petitionary prayer itself) that otherwise would be absent: for example, increased human responsibility for the nature of the world, things that happen in response to reasons generated by requests (rather than provided without requests), and enhanced relationship with God along various dimensions. Using the word in a slightly nonstandard way, I will call these *consequentialist* defenses of petitionary prayer because they appeal to the consequences of this dependency arrangement created by God, rather than to any reasons God might have that are independent of those consequences.

There are other defenses of petitionary prayer that share this same consequentialist structure but do not fall into any of the general categories mentioned so far. For example, Murray and Meyers argue that requiring petitionary prayers helps prevent idolatry and foster interdependence among believers (Murray and Meyers 1994). And Cohoe appeals to the value of petitionary prayer manifesting the character of the divine: "Petitionary prayer is a distinct way for us to cause things, by asking God for them, and, thus, it makes the causal order of things more complete and diverse, better displaying God's goodness."[55]

Like the other difference-making approaches, these defenses address the value-adding constraint by specifying some good thing the occurrence of

---

[53] See the critical discussion of some of these approaches in Davison 2017, for example.
[54] As before, it is not clear that this family of defenses can explain why God might make the provision of serious needs dependent upon petitionary prayers from third parties.
[55] Cohoe 2014, 33; for a similar answer to the question of why God created anything in the first place, see Johnston 2019.

which is contingent upon God's requiring petitionary prayers. And as before, there seems to be no way to rule out the possibility that in some cases, at least, the good things provided in this way might make the right kind of difference to God, in terms of providing a sufficiently strong reason to require the offering of petitionary prayers before the granting of some provision. However, it is not clear that the good things identified here would explain why God would not provide something good in cases where a great deal is at stake, especially for a third party, just because petitionary prayers were not offered. But this is just to repeat the theme emerging from this section, namely, that not every defense of petitionary prayer can cover every case in which people typically think that the offering of such prayers is important.

Not all defenses of petitionary prayer are consequentialist defenses in my sense of this word because some appeal to entirely different kinds of considerations; to mark the difference, I will call these *deontological* defenses instead. According to deontological defenses, God makes the provision of some good thing dependent upon the offering of petitionary prayers because somehow this is right or fitting or appropriate, regardless of whether it leads to the production of some other good thing (distinct from the object requested in the petitionary prayer itself).

For example, one way of reading Eleonore Stump's much-discussed defense involves not just the (causal) consequences of God's requiring petitionary prayers before providing things in terms of the effects this has on a personal relationship, but rather the moral permissibility of doing so. According to this reading, God properly values the freedom of creatures, so God would have reason to provide certain things only if creatures requested them, out of proper respect for creaturely autonomy.[56] This approach appeals to God's knowledge of what is right or fitting or appropriate,[57] rather than taking the consequentialist approach that involves appealing to God's deciding to provide things only if they are requested in petitionary prayer because this would produce good things (distinct from the objects requested in petitionary prayer) that otherwise would be absent.

Scott Hill offers a clearly deontological defense of petitionary prayer. In terms of my terminology, Hill's defense is also an example of a non-difference-making approach, since it is consistent with the possibility that God would have given the very same things to people even if they had not asked for them. In Hill's view, in at least some cases, people deserve to receive things that God had already decided to give them because they requested those things sincerely in

---

[56] For a detailed discussion and defense of this approach, see Davison 2017, 136–42.
[57] Where God has such reasons, they must be viewed as prima facie, or defeasible, or justifying instead of requiring; see the discussions of this question in Murphy 2017.

petitionary prayer (Hill 2018, 409). And "A world at which S receives and overall deserves x is better than an otherwise similar world at which S receives but does not overall deserve x" (Hill 2018, 408). In a similar vein, Isaac Choi argues that whereas petitionary prayers express praiseworthy attitudes, a lack of petitionary prayer often expresses morally culpable attitudes. So God's answering some petitionary prayers (and not providing some things when petitionary prayers are not offered) is part of just system of punishments and rewards (Choi 2016, 40–1).

These deontological defenses succeed in identifying a reason for God to make the provision of certain goods dependent upon the offering of petitionary prayers in some cases, but like the consequentialist defenses described previously, they do not cover the full range of cases in which people typically assume that it is reasonable to offer petitionary prayers. In particular, it is hard to see how the strength of these deontological reasons would justify God in making the provision of some serious need dependent upon the offering of petitionary prayers by a third party.[58]

As noted previously, Daniel Johnson endorses a non-difference-making defense of petitionary prayer that appeals to the general idea of involvement in God's activities as a reason people might have for offering petitionary prayers. In terms of his analogy of participation in team sports, sometimes people want to be part of the team, even if their play does not make *the* difference in the outcome of the game (see Johnson 2020, 144–6). So it is also possible to offer a consequentialist defense of petitionary prayer that does not assume a difference-making approach to the question of what it means to say that a prayer has been answered.

In this section, I have not found any single defense of petitionary prayer that clearly explains the value of petitionary prayers across the full range of cases in which people typically think that the offering of such prayers is important. In some cases, as Isaac Choi has pointed out, the good things in question would occur if people simply believed that God was answering their petitionary prayers, even if this was not in fact the case.[59] However, a number of the defenses I have considered seem to be clearly successful over a narrower range of cases. I will return to this point later when I take up practical considerations involving when to offer petitionary prayers and what to request when making them.

---

[58] For a more detailed description of which kinds of petitionary prayers seem to be rationally justifiable, based upon a different taxonomy of defenses, see Davison 2017, chapter 10.

[59] See the discussion of this placebo-like objection to parts of the Murray and Meyers defense in Choi 2016, 38.

5 Epistemology

In this section, I will explore the epistemology of petitionary prayer. I will argue that even if people know or reasonably believe that God answers petitionary prayers in general, typically people do not seem to be in a position to conclude that their prayers have been answered in specific cases.

Suppose for a moment that God exists and actually answers petitionary prayers regularly – do people ever know this, or reasonably believe it, in particular cases? Some of the defenses I have considered so far seem to depend upon an affirmative answer to this question, at least in part. For example, consider again responsibility-based defenses, according to which God sometimes requires petitionary prayers before providing certain things because it enhances human responsibility for the world. Although one need not know or even reasonably believe that one's actions will have a certain consequence before one can be responsible for that consequence to some degree, typically such knowledge or reasonable belief would increase one's responsibility. So, if people knew or reasonably believed that God would answer their prayers, this would make them more responsible for the obtaining of those states of affairs, all other things being equal.[60]

Something similar seems to hold with respect to relationship-based defenses. In order for one's relationship with God to be enhanced by God's requiring petitionary prayers before providing certain things, in the ways described by these defenses, it would certainly help if one could know or reasonably believe that God has answered one's prayers on some occasions.[61]

Do people sometimes know or reasonably believe that God has answered particular petitionary prayers? In response to some skeptical arguments, Brian Embry argues that we must distinguish two things: knowing whether God has answered some particular petitionary prayer, on the one hand, and knowing that God answers petitionary prayers for certain kinds of things, in general, on the other hand.[62] He argues that although skeptical arguments undermine our confidence concerning claims to the first kind of knowledge (concerning specific petitionary prayers in particular circumstances), they do not undermine our confidence concerning claims to the second kind of knowledge (concerning God's answering petitionary prayers in general).

Embry's argument for this conclusion involves an analogy concerning a rich benefactor who promises to help you where possible, as long as you write to ask

---

[60] See the discussions of degrees of responsibility in Howard-Snyder and Howard-Snyder 2010 and Davison 2017, chapter 7.

[61] For more on this, see Davison 2017, chapters 4 and 5 and Finley 2019, 395.

[62] Embry 2018, 138; for the skeptical arguments, see Davison 2009, 2017, chapters 4 and 5.

for help (Embry 2018, 138–9). By waiting for you to ask for help, the benefactor avoids meddling in your affairs. And although the benefactor does not promise to help you whenever you ask, there is an understanding that the benefactor will help where possible. In this case, Embry claims, you know that the benefactor helps, in general, without knowing exactly when this happens, and this is enough to ground your gratitude toward the benefactor (Embry 2018, 139–40).

Embry makes a good point: it would seem to be possible to know that in general, God answers some petitionary prayers, without knowing which ones God answers. However, at the end of his paper, he points out that nothing he has said addresses what reason there might be for religious believers to think that God answers petitionary prayers in general (Embry 2018, 40). One way for someone to believe reasonably that God answers petitionary prayers in general would be for that person to believe reasonably that God has revealed this general truth, perhaps through a prophet or through scripture. Philosophers of religion have a lot to say about this possibility, but I will not discuss it here.[63] I will grant that it seems possible for people to come to know or reasonably believe that God answers petitionary prayers in general on the basis of some kind of revelation.

Another way in which people might claim to believe reasonably that God answers petitionary prayers in general is through scientific studies designed to measure the effects of prayer across large groups of people over time in roughly the same way that we try to measure the causal influence of other forces in the world.[64] We can imagine studies designed to measure something like petitions among human beings, such as the effect of asking politicians to change policies over time, but we need to ask whether this same approach makes sense in the case of petitionary prayer to the God of theism.

If we assume that this approach does make sense, the best studies to date have turned out to be rather disappointing, showing no impressive correlation between the offering of petitionary prayers and better outcomes for medical patients.[65] So current studies do not support the claim that God answers petitionary prayers in general – in fact, they suggest that petitionary prayers make no important difference. On the other hand, a number of philosophers have argued that the usual scientific methodology that we use to measure other things is somehow misplaced here. For example, one assumption behind such studies is that differences between individuals are canceled out when the experimental and control groups are large enough, but is it safe to assume that God's reasons for healing (or not healing) individual persons would be canceled

---

[63] See the helpful discussion and references in Wahlberg 2020.

[64] These studies clearly assume what I have called here a difference-making approach to answered prayer; for a different way of describing this feature of the experiments, see Veber 2007.

[65] For example, see Harris et al. 1999 and Benson et al. 2006.

out if the groups are large enough? If they are not, then the differences we measure between the groups are not due to the effects of petitionary prayer alone, and it's hard to know how we should interpret the results. It's hard to know what to say here.[66] Either way, though, it does not seem that scientific studies lend much support to the claim that God answers petitionary prayers in general, at least with respect to the best studies conducted so far.

Another way in which someone might believe reasonably that God answers petitionary prayers, in general, would be for that person to believe reasonably that God has answered particular petitionary prayers in the past. In other places, I have argued that theists should not expect to know God's reasons for bringing about specific events and that this casts doubt on claims to know that specific events should be counted as answers to specific petitionary prayers. God's knowledge vastly surpasses ours, and God's purposes may be very long term and very complex, so we should not expect to know why God does things.[67] Embry seems to grant the force of these arguments, but not everyone does. For example, Isaac Choi argues that one can reasonably believe that specific events are answers to petitionary prayers, at least in certain circumstances, because of indirect evidence. He appeals to four considerations here: timing, specificity, internal assurance, and statistical inference (Choi 2016, 44–53). It will be helpful to examine each of these arguments carefully.

Choi describes a case introduced by Howard-Snyder (2010, 54) in which several people pray that Misty be healed from back pain at 11:05 a.m., and Misty reports the disappearance of the pain at just that time (without knowing that people were praying for this then). Choi describes four possible explanations of the disappearance of the pain then:

(a) God healed Misty at 11:05 because the others requested this in petitionary prayer at that time.

(b) God healed Misty at 11:05 because God had other reasons for doing so, at that time, reasons that were independent of the petitionary prayers offered by the others.

(c) God had other reasons for healing Misty at some time or other, reasons that were independent of the petitionary prayers offered by the others, and God randomly selected 11:05 as the time at which Misty would be healed.

(d) God did not heal Misty at all – in fact, the pain ended for natural reasons, coincidentally at 11:05, when the others were offering petitionary prayers for her healing.

---

[66] For more on this question, see the discussion in Davison 2017, chapter 5.

[67] See Davison 2009, 2017, chapters 4 and 5, Howard-Snyder 2010, and Whitcomb et al. 2017.

Notice first that there are other possible explanations that are not included in the list – the list is not exhaustive. For example, perhaps an evil nonhuman agent healed Misty in order to deceive people for some mysterious reason. Yet another possibility is that God does not exist, but Nous does, where Nous is a deity that is not quite as powerful, knowledgeable, or morally excellent as God would be, and Nous healed Misty in response to petitionary prayers directed at (the nonexistent) God. (There are countless other possible explanations that I will not try to enumerate here.) There may also be additional possible explanations "in between" those listed – for example, perhaps God healed Misty at that time both because the others requested this and because God had conclusive and independent reasons for doing so then (a combination of (a) and (b)).[68]

One of the two Howard-Snyders (the co-authors who wrote Howard-Snyder and Howard-Snyder 2010) argues that (a) is more likely than the other explanations. (The other one agrees with the view I defended in Davison [2009], according to which we are not entitled to draw this conclusion; the Howard-Snyders do not reveal which is which.) Choi agrees with the first more epistemically optimistic assessment. The timing of the events described is the first feature to which he appeals in his defense of the claim that (a) is more likely than the other explanations.

Consider first (d). Suppose we knew that a certain percentage of patients suffering from back pain would spontaneously recover, without medical intervention. This might raise the probability in our minds of Misty's pain disappearing spontaneously at some point or other. But according to Choi,

> Even if this significantly raises our estimate of the probability of the pain naturally going away during Misty's lifetime, that it happened at 11:05 on that day, right when they were praying for her, is still extremely improbable, though somewhat higher than when we thought that such spontaneous recoveries were far rarer. Compared with (a), (d) is still very much less likely. (2016, 47)

I'm not convinced that we should accept Choi's claims about the relative probabilities here.

First of all, it is not clear what kind of probability is involved. If Choi has in mind some kind of simple subjective probability, then I think we should notice that this is likely to vary significantly, depending upon background assumptions. There are clearly some persons for whom (a) is more likely than any of the other explanations, given their background beliefs. If that is supposed to be

---

[68] Here, I am not assuming that in order for God to answer a prayer, God must bring about the object of the prayer only because it was requested and for no other reason; for more on this complicated question, see Davison 2017, chapter 2.

sufficient to show that it is reasonable to believe that prayers for Misty were answered on that occasion, then I think we have here a very low threshold for what counts as reasonable. In this sense, for example, it is reasonable for many people to believe in various folktales, like the spontaneous generation of moths in closets. If that is the point, then I think we should grant it without hesitation, but I do not think it is very interesting epistemologically.[69]

If we consider instead objective probabilities, we need to know which background assumptions Choi takes for granted in order to judge the relative probabilities in question. In order to say that (d) is very much less objectively probable than (a), it seems that we need to have a fairly clear sense of the objective probability of (a) and the objective probability of (d), respectively. But I'm not sure that we do. In one sense, every particular event is highly objectively improbable when described in highly specific terms. In order to know exactly how objectively probable or improbable (d) is, we need much more information – specifically, we need information about the causes of Misty's condition, including the timing of various processes at work in the production of her pain. It is relevant to know the objective probability of spontaneous recovery in general, as Choi points out, but the objective probability that this will happen to Misty specifically depends upon a great many facts about Misty, facts to which we do not appear to have access in this case.[70]

In the same way, in order to ascertain how objectively probable or improbable (a) is, we need much more information – specifically, information about God's plans and God's reasons for acting (or not acting) in the world in Misty's situation. In general, we do not have access to those things, so it's very hard to say how objectively probable or improbable (a) is. Consider the position commonly described as skeptical theism. Although this view is highly controversial among philosophers of religion, the debate concerning it has shed renewed light on what we should expect to know concerning specific events in the world: if God exists, God is omniscient and omnipotent, and God has a providential plan for the world, then we should not expect to know why God permits specific events to occur.[71] So, even if we knew that God answered petitionary prayers regularly, it would be very hard to say how objectively probable it is that God would answer any specific petitionary prayer, which makes it very hard to say how objectively probable (a) is. These same concerns apply to (b) and (c).

---

[69] Having reasonable beliefs in this sense does not seem at all related to having knowledge, for instance, or to reasons that can be easily acquired by others through testimony.

[70] For discussion of closely related issues concerning probability assessments, see Draper 2013.

[71] See Bergmann 2009, Howard-Snyder 2010, Dougherty and McBrayer 2014, and Dougherty 2016.

I am not arguing that Choi is wrong to say that (a) is more objectively probable than any of the other explanations – for all I know, he could be right about that. But I am arguing that nobody is in a position to know or reasonably believe that (a) is more objectively probable than any of the other explanations, simply because we do not have enough information to determine how objectively probable any of these explanations are. Choi is right in saying that we often appeal to timing in order to rule out coincidences (2016, 46–7), but typically, we do this in cases where the factors that are relevant to the comparison of competing hypotheses are ones to which we have some form of reliable access, such as the breaking of a window by a baseball.[72]

Choi observes that if people had been praying on multiple occasions for Misty's recovery, as opposed to praying only once at 11:05 on the day in question, then there would be "probabilistic dilution" of the effect of timing on our estimation of the probabilities involved here (2016, 48). But he notes that this is not always the case and points to well-known examples from the Jewish and Christian scriptures involving single petitionary prayers for specific events and dramatic results following immediately. I grant the force of the evidence in such dramatic cases,[73] but such evidence seems to be the exception rather than the rule – people do not report such things very often, and the ordinary person typically does not have evidence that is anything like this.[74]

> Choi also claims that over time,
> 　　. . . if we take into account multiple instances of seeming answers to prayer that involve close matches in time, the probability that all of them are merely coincidental in their timing decreases extremely rapidly, given the multiplication of already very low probabilities (we multiply them since each seeming answer to prayer's timing is probabilistically independent of the others if they are the result of chance). So the more seeming answers to prayer I have observed that have such good timing, the more confident I can be that I have witnessed some instances when God did answer prayer. (Choi 2016, 49)

This is not a sound argument. Suppose we witness a long series of events that involve close matches in time between the offering of a petitionary prayer and the occurrence of the apparent answer. Imagine also that for each event in the series, we grant that it is objectively improbable that it is a coincidence. (I argued previously that we should not grant this assumption, but I will make it here for the sake of the argument.) Then it is true that the conjunctive claim

---

[72] This case is mentioned in Howard-Snyder and Howard-Snyder 2010, 56; see Choi 2016, 46.

[73] Assuming that they are well-documented and so on – I will not discuss here the issues raised by that dimension of the argument.

[74] For an interesting and helpful discussion of contemporary belief in miracles, see Nagasawa 2018.

that every member of the series is a coincidence will be very low and will become even lower as more members are added to the series. But it simply does not follow that this increasingly low objective probability implies a higher objective probability that some member of this same series is a case of actual petitionary prayer answered by God – instead, it raises the objective probability of the disjunction of all of the possible alternative explanations (which I would not even attempt to enumerate – as indicated previously, there are countlessly many of them).

With respect to specificity, the second source of support for indirect evidence, Choi argues that:

> As the specificity of a prayer increases, it becomes far less likely that an event would match in all the details by chance. And as a prayer's specificity increases, it also becomes far less likely that God would, for reasons wholly independent from that prayer, choose to bring about precisely that outcome. Compared with such incredibly improbable coincidences, it becomes far more likely that God answered the prayer. (Choi 2016, 49)

By way of example here, he describes a person praying specifically for a house for rent: a white house with a white picket fence, a grassy front yard, within two or three miles from the campus, for no more than a specific amount of money per month. Soon thereafter, this person discovered just such a house for rent (Choi 2016, 49).

As before, assuming we are talking about objective probabilities, I am hesitant to endorse Choi's claims because I doubt whether we have access to all of the relevant information. For example, it is possible that God has plans for this person that involve that specific house, but not because it happened to match the features that were mentioned in the petitionary prayer. Or God might have reasons that involve other persons or other states of affairs that are served by this arrangement specifically, even though we have no idea what they are. Unless we can assign some probability to these other possibilities, it seems impossible to make the claim that Choi makes, which involves comparing the probability that God would bring about this specific outcome for reasons wholly independent from the petitionary prayer, on the one hand, and the probability that God answered the petitionary prayer by finding a house that matched those specific features, on the other hand.

To his credit, Choi admits that highly improbable events do happen, and so "chance events are bound to match up with specific prayers" once in a while (Choi 2016, 50). I think this is an important fact to consider in connection with the phenomenon of specificity – sometimes, there are genuine coincidences, after all. If people are looking for matches between their petitionary prayers and what happens in the world, they are bound to find them over time, and some form of confirmation bias probably explains why they remember those cases and do not remember cases in which no match is found.

But Choi also makes a point of arguing that we should not overestimate the importance of the possibility of coincidence in connection with apparently answered petitionary prayer:

> However, if the probability of the chance hypothesis gets too low, alternative non-chance hypotheses become far more plausible. A woman winning a large jackpot lottery is a relatively everyday occurrence. But if the same woman wins three or four multi-million-dollar lotteries over a period of several years, some kind of fraud perpetrated with the help of insiders becomes the likelier explanation. (Choi 2016, 50)

I'm not confident that this analogy is helpful. In the imaginary case of the woman winning multiple lotteries, we have confident estimations of the objective probabilities involved. But in the case of alternative explanations like (a)–(d) listed previously, in connection with Misty's recovery, we do not have such estimations.

Choi's appeal to specificity reminds me of the sorts of tests one might employ to decide whether someone is reliable in predicting the future. Specific predictions that came true would provide more evidence than general ones, certainly. And the more successful predictions a person made, the more evidence we would have for the conclusion that the person is a reliable guide to the future. This suggests that if we really wanted stronger evidence for the conclusion that petitionary prayer is effective, then we should offer more specific petitionary prayers. But that approach raises a number of issues, to be discussed in Section 6.

Third, Choi mentions internal assurance, the idea that God might directly give a person "the impression or belief that God has acted or will act in response (or has denied the request)" (Choi 2016, 51), and recommends Alvin Plantinga's account of the internal testimony of the Holy Spirit as a helpful model here.[75] I agree with Choi that God could directly produce in a created person a true belief to the effect that something happening in the world is an answer to petitionary prayer, along with a feeling of certainty and assurance. However, I do not think that any theistic religious traditions claim that this typically happens when petitionary prayers are answered.[76] Also, in the same way that

---

[75] See Plantinga 2000 and Choi 2016, 52.

[76] Daniel Johnson has pointed out to me (in personal correspondence) that some strains of Christianity teach that we have both natural tendencies and divine prompts designed to enable us to recognize certain events in the world as divine actions and that some of these cases might involve answered petitionary prayer (e.g., in the case of experiences of forgiveness); there is more to explore along these lines, but I do not have the space to discuss it here.

Choi knows personally several people who have claimed to receive internal assurances that their petitionary prayers have been or will be answered (Choi 2016, 52), I know personally many examples of people who claim to have experienced the very same things repeatedly, only to be later disappointed by the discovery that what they had specifically requested in petitionary prayer had in fact not come to pass. It is not at all clear that people can reliably tell from the inside, so to speak, whether such feelings of assurance are reliable in particular cases.[77]

Before turning to Choi's fourth argument, it might be helpful to return to the non-difference-making approach to answered petitionary prayer introduced by Johnson previously, which promises to solve the epistemological problem here rather neatly. Suppose that God is omnirational in Pruss's sense so that God acts on all unexcluded reasons, and imagine that my offering of a petitionary prayer for something counts as one of those reasons. Suppose also that God brings about the thing I requested, on the basis of all of God's unexcluded reasons for doing so. Then my offering of the prayer was among God's reasons for doing so, which implies that this should be counted as a case of answered petitionary prayer.[78]

In order for me to know that this is the case, though, several things need to be in place. First, I must know that God exists and that God is omnirational in Pruss's sense. The epistemic standing I possess for my belief that God has answered my particular petitionary prayer cannot rise above the level of epistemic standing that I possess for these other two beliefs.[79] In addition, if God has conclusive reasons for bringing about the thing I requested that are completely independent of my petitionary prayer, it is not clear to me that we should really count this as a case of answered petitionary prayer.[80] So it is not obvious that an appeal to omnirationality can bridge the epistemological gap here.

The fourth argument Choi develops here concerns the teachings of specific religious traditions:

> Since people believe that God keeps his promises, even if they did not have
> a very reliable method of determining whether God has answered prayer in
> a given instance, they can still infer from such promises that at least some

---

[77] As Sabrina Little has pointed out to me (in conversation), though, some people might be better than others in terms of distinguishing genuine internal assurances from apparent ones. Daniel Johnson has noted (in correspondence) that my point here raises questions about the internalism/externalism debate in epistemology; for a discussion of the epistemology of petitionary prayer that does not assume internalism, see Davison 2017, chapters 4 and 5.

[78] Thanks to Daniel Johnson for clarifying this connection (in correspondence).

[79] Thanks to Daniel and Frances Howard-Snyder for pointing this out to me (in correspondence).

[80] For further discussion and arguments to the contrary, see Davison 2017, chapter 2 and Johnson 2020.

percentage of seemingly answered prayers are actually answered. If a believer reflects back on all the prayers that she thought were answered by God, she can at least make a statistical inference that it is very likely that many if not most of the best candidates of instances of answered prayer (judged by her own lights, perhaps those that had the most profound impact on those for whom she prayed and on her own faith) were in fact answered prayers. If she knows or is justified in believing her faith's teachings on prayer, then she also knows or is justified in believing the conclusion of this inference. (Choi 2016, 52–3)[81]

Once again, I am skeptical about this inference. It seems to me that even if a religious believer holds that God answers petitionary prayers in general, it would be a mistake to expect to be able to identify any of them. It might be helpful to consider this from two different points of view.

From the point of view of someone who is skeptical about whether specific petitionary prayers have been answered, it would not be surprising for many people to find regular matches between fervent prayers and various outcomes in the world, as long as people are looking for them. But because we don't have enough information about God's reasons for acting or the conditions in the world that led to the events we observe, such correlations typically do not provide strong evidence of the kind of connection needed for answered petitionary prayer.

From the point of view of the sincere and confident religious believer, there is another reason for doubting this inference. Kate Finley has pointed out that sometimes, we are inclined to count something as an answer to petitionary prayer even though it fails to correspond to the details of the actual request. In addition, sometimes we are inclined not to count something as an answer to petitionary prayer, even if it matches our request, because it turns out to be very different from what we expected it to be.[82] If this is right, then God might in fact answer one's petitionary prayers by doing things in the world that one could never recognize as answers to them, simply because one doesn't have enough information. I doubt many religious persons would find these conclusions objectionable at all – few would be surprised to discover, in an afterlife, that their prayers had been answered in such ways, that they were wrong about the ways in which they thought their prayers had been answered in this life, or that very few of their prayers had been answered at all, for various reasons.

In this section, I have argued that even if it is granted that people know or reasonably believe that God answers petitionary prayers, in general, typically

---

[81] See also the discussion of the importance of religious traditions in Cohoe 2018.
[82] Finley 2019, 393–4.

people do not seem to be in a position to conclude that their prayers have been answered in specific cases.

6 Practical Considerations and Quasi-Petitionary Prayer

In this section, I will ask some practical questions about petitionary prayer that lead us in new directions.

Earlier I considered a number of defenses of petitionary prayer, along with some of their advantages and limitations. In specific cases, it might be impossible to know whether one or more of these defenses applies to one's situation, especially if one must make a decision about what to do given limits of time and resources. People seem to consider offering petitionary prayers only in cases in which they have limited or no control over a given outcome, where the outcome matters to them.[83] People also seem to offer prayers in cases in which it seems that more than one outcome is possible. This might explain the case I mentioned at the beginning of this Element: perhaps I did not think to pray for my sister's recovery because it seemed impossible given what I knew about this situation, whereas my wife's medical situation seemed to me to be undetermined because of what I didn't know about that situation.

Should people offer petitionary prayers whenever there is something significant at stake over which they have little control because, for all they know, they might be in a situation in which God expects them to do so? Assuming some kind of difference-making approach, Stump suggests that the answer here might be "yes":

> As lon as a believer is not in a position to know which states of affairs are divinely determined to occur regardless of prayers, there is some point in petitionary prayer—any given case may be one in which God would not have brought about the desired state of affairs without prayer for it.
>
> (Stump 1979, 404)

Stump's argument here is essentially an appeal to ignorance, which always cuts both ways.[84] But maybe it can be strengthened by what I will call a "combination defense." According to this approach, even though no single defense of petitionary prayer provides a conclusive reason for offering petitionary prayers on a given occasion because it is not clear whether the conditions it describes actually obtain, the fact that there are so many of these partially successful defenses provides us with a reason to offer petitionary prayers, just in case.

---

[83] People do not ask God to pass the salt, for instance (Davison 2009, 303, fn. 41).

[84] For a similar argument, see Parker and Rettler 2017, 183.

The situation here could be compared to a case in which you are deciding whether to apply for a job based upon an advertisement when it is not clear to you whether you fully satisfy any of the criteria listed for the position. Suppose that you do have some qualifications in each area, you need a job, and the cost of applying for the job is low. In this case, you might apply in the hopes that some combination of your credentials will be sufficient, in the circumstances, to move the potential employer to hire you, without knowing which of your credentials would be doing the work, so to speak.

This combination defense of petitionary prayer dovetails nicely with what I have elsewhere called the "wager defense" of petitionary prayer, which suggests that it is rational to pray in this way when the cost of doing so is minimal and there is something significant at stake.[85] The basic idea is similar to the well-known argument called Pascal's wager, according to which one should take actions likely to produce belief in God because of the expected utility of this over the long term.[86]

Of course, if we are attentive to the world around us, we are constantly faced with significant possible outcomes over which we have little direct control. So, if we were to pray in the petitionary way whenever we became aware of one of these situations, we might literally do nothing else. And that would not be rational because it would require us to neglect the many other things we are required to do. The combination defense and wager defense bring sharply into focus another practical question: for what exactly should we pray?

It is commonly assumed that God would answer prayers only for good things.[87] But which good things should be requested in petitionary prayer in a given situation? And is it important that one's petitionary prayers have specific objects in the first place? It is one thing to know that a situation is not going well, but as we will see later, it is quite another thing to know what would actually make the situation better. This consideration generates pressure in the direction of very general petitionary prayers, like "Thy will be done," which express a general desire for things to go well. (I will say more about this prayer later.)

I noted previously that Choi appeals to the specificity of petitionary prayers as indirect evidence for the conclusion that such prayers have been answered by God when the things requested come to pass. He mentions an example in which a person prayed specifically for a white house with a white picket fence and a grassy front yard for rent, within two or three miles from a university campus, for no more than a certain amount of money per month. Why would people offer

---

[85] For more on this argument, see Davison 2017, 147–8.

[86] This argument is typically attributed to Blaise Pascal (1623–1662); see Mawson 2010 and Hájek 2018.

[87] See the interesting discussion of petitionary prayers for bad things in Smilansky 2012.

such specific prayers? Is it because they have in mind a specific arrangement that would make them happy? Should people be encouraged to offer such specific prayers, perhaps by first trying to figure out what things would be good if they came to be?

I have several hesitations here. First, this approach seems importantly similar to activities designed to test God, which is often forbidden in traditional theistic religious traditions. Although there are examples from these traditions in which paradigm figures are praised for using some kind of test to obtain information from God,[88] there are also warnings when such tests reflect doubts or threaten to undermine faith if they don't turn out well. This danger might be especially pressing for those who hold that the evidence of answered petitionary prayer is a significant part of their reason for believing that God exists.

Second, this approach seems to suggest that our own personal beliefs about what would be good in a given situation are likely to be reliable, which seems dubious. Although we have lots of beliefs about what would be good for us in a given situation, especially in the short term, we are often unaware of the unintended consequences of our own actions and the actions of others, and this is even more true over the long term. Simone Weil offers an interesting commentary on "Forgive us our debts, as we also forgive our debtors," a line from the so-called Lord's Prayer from the Christian tradition. She argues that we typically assume that based on our past efforts, the universe owes us particular good things in the future.[89] But, in saying this line in the prayer, we renounce all claims to the future:

> In renouncing at one stroke all the fruits of the past without exception, we can ask of God that our past sins may not bear their miserable fruits of evil and error. So long as we cling to the past, God himself cannot stop this horrible fruiting. We cannot hold on to the past without retaining our crimes, for we are unaware of what is most essentially bad in us.[90]

Weil's commentary adds a different dimension to the common phrase, "Be careful what you wish for – you just might get it."

Finally, some have argued that highly specific prayers might actually convey a lack of trust in God because they suggest that God needs specific prompting in order to be moved to act. (I will explore this idea in more detail later.) So, even if Choi is right in saying that there are cases in which very specific prayers seem to

---

[88] Thanks to Daniel and Frances Howard-Snyder for reminding me of this fact.

[89] She also notes that "The near approach of death is horrible chiefly because it forces the knowledge upon us that these compensations will never come": Weil 1959, 175.

[90] Weil 1959, 174–5; see also the discussion of Weil in Phillips 1981, 69–70. For the textual origins of the Lord's Prayer in the Christian gospels, see Matthew 6:9–13 and Luke 11:2–4.

be answered, for a number of reasons, it is not clear that people should be encouraged to replicate the pattern of offering specific petitionary prayers.[91]

Moving even further in this direction, Allison Thornton has argued recently that we should not want to make a difference to God's action through petitionary prayer (Thornton, under review). Thornton helps explain her argument by appealing to a helpful example:

> Suppose you broke your arm. You would like to recover fully, but before you attempt to bring it about, you might ask yourself, "What would God like for me?" knowing that what God wants for you is a function of both God's omniscience and love for you and consequently is truly what is best for you. After all, God knows what your preferences are, what your weaknesses and strengths are, what you need to flourish, etc., and God has perfect love for you . . .. Thus, your preference for recovery should be provisional, contingent on whatever God's preferences are. Moreover, God knows and loves not only you, but everyone else as well . . .. God knows the price of each good and which prices are worth paying. Your preference for recovery should be contingent on God's preferences about these more global facts, too. To the extent that you can, you ought to align your preferences with God's, even when they fail to favor you in particular. (Thornton, under review)

Thornton argues then that if your recovery is part of every future that God regards as sufficiently worthy of creation (she calls these "satisficing futures") and you know this, then any petitionary prayer you offer for your own recovery would be not only superfluous but not even really petitionary. This is because the point of petitionary prayer is to make some difference to God, based on the nature of the thing requested, but in the scenario we have described, you would know that your recovery will happen whether or not you pray for it.

On the other hand, if you know that your recovery is part of no future that God regards as worthy of creation, then you should not want to recover because God knows best, so you should not ask for this. Finally, if your recovery is part of some futures that God regards as worthy of creation, but not others, then you should not try to influence God's choice either – for example, if God is neutral about your recovery, then you should be neutral, too. So, whether your recovery is part of every future that God regards as worthy of creation, or none of them, or some of them, you have no relevant reason, based on the value of the target of your petitionary prayer, to try to influence God's preferences.

Thornton's argument is worthy of further consideration.[92] Notice that it focuses on the nature of the object requested by the petitioner in petitionary

---

[91] A similar point has been made in connection with Flint's claim that petitionary prayer can be used to "raise the stakes" in a given situation: see Davison 2009, 294.

[92] I have summarized her argument very briefly here and omitted many important details.

prayer, which she calls the "target." As mentioned previously, Kate Finley has pointed out that typical debates concerning petitionary prayer probably focus too much on this element; her argument for this conclusion is important for us to consider carefully. She imagines a pair of cases that differ in interesting respects. In the first case, S prays for her mother to be healed, and God grants this request, but only after thirty years of suffering, and S's mother dies soon thereafter. This doesn't really seem like an answer to S's prayer, even though technically it satisfies the criteria we typically apply here.[93]

In Finley's second case, S prays for a job as a teacher because S believes it would be fulfilling. If God granted the request but it was not fulfilling, after all, we would have hesitations about saying that the request was granted; what if God instead provided S a job as an artist, which S then found very fulfilling? Here, it seems that if God honors the intention or motivation that lies behind the petitionary prayer, then that should count as a case of answered prayer, despite failing to satisfy our usual criteria.[94]

If Finley is right in thinking that God's honoring the intention behind a petitionary prayer is more important than God's actually bringing about the target, then perhaps we should not worry so much about trying to identify a suitable target in the first place, which would help resolve the practical problem concerning what to pray for in the petitionary way. If I pray for X because I think it will lead to Y, and Y is what seems most important to me in the situation that prompted my prayer, then maybe I need not worry so much about whether X will really lead to Y – having expressed what I really care about, I can leave the rest to God, so to speak. This line of inquiry leads us to a new and interesting possibility that has been largely overlooked in the literature to date: petitionary prayers without requests involving objects or targets at all.

A few years ago, I was camping in the remote Michigan wilderness, many miles from civilization, when I discovered that I didn't know where my twelve-year-old son Andrew was.[95] After searching for some time and noticing the onset of darkness approaching rapidly, I began to fear for his safety. Out of desperation, I prayed for his safe return. This was a clear case of petitionary prayer, with a token of request directed at God, a specific object or target, and all of the other elements that one typically associates with paradigm cases.[96] But imagine that things had gone slightly differently: suppose that everything else

---

[93] See Finley 2019, 393–4.

[94] Finley 2019, 394; see also the discussion of luck, responsibility, and interrupted prayer in Davison 2017, chapter 7.

[95] For a more detailed description of this event, including the outcome, see Davison 2017, 1.

[96] See the discussion of the elements of petitionary prayer in Davison 2017, chapter 2.

was the same, except that I did not actually ask God to do anything in particular in that situation. I will call this a "quasi-petitionary prayer."

In quasi-petitionary prayer, as I am using this term, nearly all of the elements involved in ordinary petitionary prayer are present: the prayer is directed to God; there is some situation or concern that is the focus of the prayer; and there is the intention to focus upon that situation or concern with God, so to speak, in the hope that God not only knows everything about it but also cares, at least to some extent, for the same things we care about. But there is no petition involving an object or target, no request at all. In quasi-petitionary prayer, as I understand it here, there is simply no attempt to make a difference with respect to God's action in the world.

It is interesting to note that quasi-petitionary prayer could be defended in many of the same ways that petitionary prayer is defended in the literature. Consider first the difference-making approach and responsibility-based defenses. If God were to return my son to safety in the Michigan wilderness in response to my quasi-petitionary prayer and God would not have done this had I not engaged in quasi-petitionary prayer, then I might very well have additional responsibility for the nature of the world, in the same way in which I would in a clear case of answered petitionary prayer.

According to request-based defenses of petitionary prayer, requesting some-thing from God generates a new reason for God to bring it about, thereby making a difference. In quasi-petitionary prayer, as I have defined it, there is no such request, so the same mechanism cannot be at work. But there is a different mechanism at work instead. When a person shares their deepest concerns with another, even if they do not ask for help, this constitutes an invitation for the second person to adopt those same concerns also. In the case of quasi-petitionary prayer, typically we imagine that God already shares the same con-cerns as the petitioner, for everyone and everything involved in the situation that prompted the prayer, so this invitation might well be redundant. But the sharing invitation itself can also generate a new reason for God to act in that situation, in the same way that such sharing invitations generate reasons among human beings.

Finally, consider relationship-based defenses of petitionary prayer. Clearly turning to God in quasi-petitionary prayer could enhance one's relationship with God, even if one never knew whether such prayer made a difference in the situations that prompted it. And this might give God a reason to provide certain things, such as a sense of the divine presence, only if they are prompted by something like quasi-petitionary prayer.[97]

---

[97] For more on a related topic, see the discussion of the so-called autonomy defense of petitionary prayer in Davison 2017, 136–42. It is worth noting that defenses of quasi-petitionary prayer need not explain why God would make the provision of some highly consequential good to a third-

Non-difference-making defenses are also relevant here. As Johnson pointed out, sometimes the goal in petitionary prayer is not to change God's mind or influence God's action in some specific way, but rather just to be involved in God's activities. This is even more clear in connection with quasi-petitionary prayer, where no specific request is involved. To return to Johnson's analogy with team sports, sometimes we want to be part of the team that wins the game, even if our own contribution was not needed for that outcome. Quasi-petitionary prayer can be a way of joining God's team, one might say.

Choi argues that the regular offering of petitionary prayers will typically lead to confirmed cases of answered prayer, which will typically lead to additional trust and faith in God, which will typically lead to new petitionary prayers: "This sets up a virtuous cycle, an amplifying feedback mechanism, with increasing trust and faith."[98] I expressed skepticism previously about the second step of this feedback loop, in connection with the epistemology of answered petitionary prayer. But, as Choi has reminded us in criticizing other defenses by appealing to something like a placebo effect, sometimes what matters is that people believe that their prayers have been answered, even if that is not actually true (Choi 2016, 38). I am sure that Choi's "virtuous cycle" describes the experiences of some persons of sincere faith.

Quasi-petitionary prayer may not always lead to increased faith in God, but it does seem to express faith in some sense, and perhaps in a different way that petitionary prayer might. In quasi-petitionary prayer, someone approaches God with the trust that God shares the same concerns that prompted the prayer. One does not request that God do anything specifically in quasi-petitionary prayer, of course, but this could be an expression of trust in God – by not asking for anything, one might be expressing confidence in God's providence, as Thornton describes in her essay (discussed previously). Let me explain.

Sometimes people argue that a lack of petitionary prayer typically betrays a lack of trust in God (e.g., see Choi 2016, 60). Perhaps this is so since most people who do not pray in the petitionary way are not religious people. But, in some cases, petitionary prayers might actually reflect a lack of trust in God. I have in mind here cases in which people appear to be trying to

---

party dependent upon the offering of quasi-petitionary prayers – this issue seemed to be the Achilles' heel for the defenses discussed in Section 3. This approach also offers an alternative for defenders of Timeless Eternity or Simple Foreknowledge who feel trapped by the challenge to petitionary prayer explored in Section 1.

[98] Choi 2016, 43; this should probably be considered a version of a relationship-based defense of petitionary prayer.

persuade God to do something through repetition, emotional appeals, and highly specific requests. In some of these cases, such an approach probably reflects the fear that if God is not informed, reminded, or repeatedly prompted, then God will not respond, and this seems to indicate a lack of faith in God.[99] By not asking God to do anything in quasi-petitionary prayer, one might be expressing confidence in God's providence.[100]

It is also worth noting that in practice, the distinctions I have drawn between the various types of prayer are likely to become blurred to the extent that they cease to be very useful. For example, Daniel Howard-Snyder reports uttering the following prayer while being charged by a bear at 3:20 a.m. while camping near Park Lake in the Central Cascade mountains: "AAAHHHHHHH!!! @#$%!!! Help!" (Howard-Snyder 2010, 44). Sometimes, people pray in ways that are difficult to classify, and that's just what we might expect. For instance, prayers of gratitude/thanks regarding the past might be parts of petitionary prayers for the future; prayers of adoration/praise might be parts of petitionary prayers, especially in public; and prayers of lamentation/complaint lead naturally to petitionary prayers for relief. In some cases, it might be impossible to fit a given prayer into these categories very neatly.

It is also common in many religious traditions to pray that God's will be done, but it is not clear that this is always a petitionary prayer. In one sense of God's will, namely, that which God will bring about no matter what, it seems pointless to pray in the petitionary way for God's will to be done. In a weaker sense of God's will, namely, that which God would prefer for the world, the petitioner seems to be expressing a commitment to advance the good and align one's values with God's, but not necessarily asking for God to do something. As Simone Weil suggests, sometimes these words simply express a willingness to accept whatever comes next.[101] So "Thy will be done" may be a quasi-petitionary prayer for many people on many occasions.[102]

---

[99] Daniel Johnson reminded me (in personal correspondence) that Jesus is described as admonishing his followers in this way: "And when you pray, do not keep on babbling like pagans, for they think they will be heard because of their many words" (Matthew 6:7).

[100] For an extended discussion of the relationship between petitionary prayer, trust, and risk, see Davison 2017, 154–9.

[101] See Weil 1959, 174–5, Phillips 1981, and Davison 2017, chapter 5 and 151–2.

[102] Caleb Cohoe has pointed out (in personal correspondence) that the idea of quasi-petitionary prayer discussed here has interesting affinities with the Stoic idea of willing the future existence of generally preferred things in a conditional way, or with reservation; for a fascinating discussion of this idea in Epictetus, see Salles 2012. As Scott Hill and Daniel and Frances Howard-Snyder have pointed out to me (in correspondence), there are also conditional petitions, like the one attributed to Jesus during the night before his crucifixion: "Father, if you are willing, take this cup from me; yet not my will, but yours be done" (Luke 22:42).

7 Conclusion

We have seen that the philosophical issues involved in prayer are numerous, complicated, and fascinating. Philosophers have argued in various ways that it is reasonable to offer petitionary prayers to God, assuming that God exists, with varying degrees of success. There are also practical considerations that suggest that it is reasonable to do this if the costs are minimal when compared to the possible benefits or when one suspects that one or more of the philosophical defenses might be in play. There are also puzzles about petitionary prayer, including what to pray for and whether it makes sense to want to influence God's action in the world. For some, quasi-petitionary prayer represents an alternative to petitionary prayer that addresses many of these concerns.

Although the contemporary philosophical debate about prayer is not very old, it seems to be gaining steam. There is every reason to expect that it will continue for some time and yield new and interesting perspectives on the issues discussed here. I have tried to feature most of the newer discussions here and to point the reader in directions that merit further consideration. I hope that this brief treatment of the issues encourages others to join in the debate.

References

Adams, Marilyn McCord and Kretzmann, Norman (1983). *Predestination, God's Foreknowledge, and Future Contingents*. Indianapolis, IN: Hackett.

Anscombe, Elizabeth (1956). Aristotle and the Sea Battle. *Mind* 65(257), 1–15.

Aristotle (2014). *Nicomachean Ethics*. Translated by C. D. C. Reeve. Indianapolis, IN: Hackett.

Basinger, David (1983). Why Petition an Omnipotent, Omniscient, Wholly Good God? *Religious Studies* 19(1), 25–41.

Benson, Herbert, Dusek, Jeffrey A., Sherwood, Jane B. et al. (2006). Study of the Therapeutic Effects of Intercessory Prayer (STEP) in Cardiac Bypass Patients: A Multicenter Randomized Trial of Uncertainty and Certainty of Receiving Intercessory Prayer. *American Heart Journal* 151(4), 934–42.

Bergmann, Michael (2009). Skeptical Theism and the Problem of Evil. In Thomas P. Flint and Michael Rea (eds.), *Oxford Handbook of Philosophical Theology*. Oxford: Oxford University Press, 375–99.

Bergmann, Michael and Cover, Jan (2006). Divine Responsibility without Divine Freedom. *Faith and Philosophy* 23(4), 381–408.

Borland, Tully (2017). Omniscience and Divine Foreknowledge. In Matthew Braddock (ed.), *Internet Encyclopedia of Philosophy*. www.iep.utm.edu /omnisci/.

Brümmer, Vincent (2008). *What Are We Doing When We Pray? On Prayer and the Nature of Faith*. Aldershot: Ashgate.

Choi, Isaac (2016). Is Petitionary Prayer Superfluous? In Jonathan Kvanvig (ed.), *Oxford Studies in Philosophy of Religion*. Oxford: Oxford University Press, 168–95.

Cohoe, Caleb (2014). God, Causality, and Petitionary Prayer. *Faith and Philosophy* 31(1), 24–35.

Cohoe, Caleb (2018). How Could Prayer Make a Difference? Discussion of Scott A. Davison, Petitionary Prayer: A Philosophical Investigation. *European Journal for Philosophy of Religion* 10, 171–85.

Cupit, Geoffrey (1994). How Requests (and Promises) Create Obligations. *Philosophical Quarterly* 44, 439–55.

Davison, Scott A. (1991). Foreknowledge, Middle Knowledge, and "Nearby" Worlds.' *International Journal for Philosophy of Religion* 30(1), 29–44.

Davison, Scott A. (2009). Petitionary Prayer. In Michael Rea and Thomas P. Flint (eds.), *The Oxford Handbook of Philosophical Theology*. Oxford: Oxford University Press, 286–305.

Davison, Scott A. (2017). *Petitionary Prayer: A Philosophical Investigation.* Oxford: Oxford University Press.

Davison, Scott A. (2018). Requests and Responses: Reply to Cohoe. *European Journal for Philosophy of Religion* 10(2), 187–94.

Davison, Scott A. (2021a). Prayer. In Stewart Goetz and Charles Taliaferro (eds.), *Wiley-Blackwell Encyclopedia of Philosophy of Religion.* Hoboken: John Wiley, 1963–70.

Davison, Scott A. (2021b). Prayer. In James Turner and James Arcadi (eds.), *T&T Clark Companion to Analytic Theology.* London: Bloomsbury, 489–97.

Davison, Scott A. (2021c). Randomness, Causation, and Divine Responsibility. In Kelly James Clark and Jeffrey Koperski (eds.), *Abrahamic Reflections on Randomness and Providence.* New York: Palgrave Macmillan, 357–74.

Davison, Scott A. (2022). Petitionary Prayer and Pride. In James Arcadi, Jordan Wessling, and Oliver Crisp (eds.), *Analyzing Prayer: Theological and Philosophical Essays.* Oxford: Oxford University Press.

Deng, Natalja (2018). Eternity in Christian Thought. In E. N. Zalta (ed.), *The Stanford Encyclopedia of Philosophy.* https://plato.stanford.edu/archives/fall2018/entries/eternity.

Dennett, Daniel C. (1984). *Elbow Room: The Varieties of Free Will Worth Wanting.* Cambridge, MA: MIT Press.

Di Muzio, Gianluca (2018). A Collaborative Model of Petitionary Prayer. *Religious Studies* 54(1), 37–54.

Dougherty, Trent (2016). Skeptical Theism. In E. N. Zalta (ed.), *The Stanford Encyclopedia of Philosophy.* https://plato.stanford.edu/archives/win2016/entries/skeptical-theism.

Dougherty, Trent and McBrayer, Justin P. (2014). *Skeptical Theism: New Essays.* Oxford: Oxford University Press.

Draper, Paul (2013). The Limitations of Pure Skeptical Theism. *Res Philosophica* 90(1), 97–111.

Ekstrom, Laura (2021). *God, Suffering, and the Value of Free Will.* Oxford: Oxford University Press.

Embry, Brian (2018). On (Not) Believing That God Has Answered a Prayer. *Faith and Philosophy* 35(1), 132–41.

Falcon, Andrea (2019). Aristotle on Causality. In E. N. Zalta (ed.), *The Stanford Encyclopedia of Philosophy.* https://plato.stanford.edu/entries/aristotle-causality.

Finley, Kate (2019). Review of Davison, Scott A. (2017). *Faith and Philosophy* 36(3), 390–5.

Fischer, John Martin and Ravizza, Mark (1998). *Responsibility and Control: A Theory of Moral Responsibility.* Cambridge: Cambridge University Press.

Flint, Thomas P. (1998). *Divine Providence: The Molinist Account*. Ithaca, NY: Cornell University Press.

Frankfurt, Harry G. (1969). Alternative Possibilities and Moral Responsibility. *Journal of Philosophy* 66, 829–39. Reprinted in Frankfurt, Harry G. (1988). *The Importance of What We Care About*. Cambridge: Cambridge University Press, 1–10.

Franks, W. Paul (2009). Why a Believer Could Believe that God Answers Prayers. *Sophia* 48(3), 319–24.

Furlong, Peter (2019). *The Challenges of Divine Determinism: A Philosophical Analysis*. Cambridge: Cambridge University Press.

Hájek, Alan (2018). Pascal's Wager. In E. N. Zalta (ed.), *The Stanford Encyclopedia of Philosophy*. https://plato.stanford.edu/archives/sum2018/entries/pascal-wager/.

Harris, William S., Gowda, Manohar, Kolb, Jerry W. et al. (1999). A Randomized, Controlled Trial of the Effects of Remote, Intercessory Prayer on Outcomes in Patients Admitted to the Coronary Care Unit. *Archives of Internal Medicine* 159(19), 2273–8.

Hasker, William (1989). *God, Time and Knowledge*. Ithaca, NY: Cornell University Press.

Hasker, William (2009). Why Simple Foreknowledge Is Still Useless (In Spite of David Hunt and Alex Pruss). *Journal of the Evangelical Theological Society* 52(3), 537–44.

Helm, Paul. (2014). Eternity. In E. N. Zalta (ed.), *The Stanford Encyclopedia of Philosophy*. https://plato.stanford.edu/cgi-bin/encyclopedia/archinfo.cgi?entry=eternity.

Hill, Scott (2018). Aquinas and Gregory the Great on the Puzzle of Petitionary Prayer. *Ergo* 5(15), 407–18.

Howard-Snyder, Daniel (2010). Epistemic Humility, Arguments from Evil, and Moral Skepticism. In Jonathan L. Kvanvig (ed.), *Oxford Studies in Philosophy of Religion* vol. 2. Oxford: Oxford University Press, 17–57.

Howard-Snyder, Daniel and Howard-Snyder, Frances (2010). The Puzzle of Petitionary Prayer. *European Journal for Philosophy of Religion* 2(2), 43–68.

Hunt, David P. (2009). The Providential Advantage of Divine Foreknowledge. In Kevin Timpe (ed.), *Arguing About Religion*. New York: Routledge, 374–85.

Johnson, Daniel M. (2020). How Puzzles of Petitionary Prayer Solve Themselves: Divine Omnirationality, Interest-Relative Explanation, and Answered Prayer. *Faith and Philosophy* 37(2), 137–57.

Johnston, Mark (2019). Why Did the One Not Remain within Itself? In Lara Buchak, Dean W. Zimmerman, and Philip Swenson (eds.), *Oxford*

Studies in Philosophy of Religion vol. 9. Oxford: Oxford University Press, 106–64.

Kane, Robert (1998). *The Significance of Free Will*. Oxford: Oxford University Press.

Kraay, Klaas (2020). *Does God Matter? Essays on the Axiological Consequences of Theism*. New York: Routledge.

Mawson, Tim J. (2005). Freedom, Human and Divine. *Religious Studies* 41(1), 55–69.

Mawson, Tim J. (2007). Praying for Known Outcomes. *Religious Studies* 43(1), 71–87.

Mawson, Tim J. (2010). Praying to Stop Being an Atheist. *International Journal for Philosophy of Religion* 67(3), 173–86.

McGrew, Timothy (2019). Miracles. In E. N. Zalta (ed.), *The Stanford Encyclopedia of Philosophy*. https://plato.stanford.edu/archives/spr2019/entries/miracles/.

Molina, Luis de (2004). *On Divine Foreknowledge: Part IV of the Concordia*. Translated by Alfred J. Freddoso. Ithaca, NY: Cornell University Press.

Mooney, Justin and Grafton-Cardwell, Patrick (under review). The Problem of Unanswered Prayer.

Murphy, Mark (2017). *God's Own Ethics*. Oxford: Oxford University Press.

Murray, Michael J. and Meyers, Kurt (1994). Ask and It Will Be Given to You. *Religious Studies* 30(3), 311–30.

Nagasawa, Yujin (2017). *Maximal God: A New Defence of Perfect Being Theism*. Oxford: Oxford University Press.

Nagasawa, Yujin (2018). *Miracles*. Oxford: Oxford University Press.

Parker, Ryan Matthew and Rettler, Bradley (2017). A Possible Worlds Solution to the Puzzle of Petitionary Prayer. *European Journal for Philosophy of Religion* 9, 179–86.

Pereboom, Derk (2001). *Living without Free Will*. Cambridge: Cambridge University Press.

Pereboom, Derk (2014). *Free Will, Agency, and Meaning in Life*. Oxford: Oxford University Press.

Phillips, Dewi Zephaniah (1981). *The Concept of Prayer*. New York: Seabury.

Pickup, Martin (2018). Answers to Our Prayers: The Unsolved but Solvable Problem of Petitionary Prayer. *Faith and Philosophy* 35, 84–104.

Plantinga, Alvin (2000). *Warranted Christian Belief*. Oxford: Oxford University Press.

Pruss, Alexander R. (2007). Prophecy without Middle Knowledge. *Faith and Philosophy* 24(4), 433–57.

Pruss, Alexander R. (2013). Omnirationality. *Res Philosophica* 90(1), 1–21.

Rice, Rebekah L. H. (2016). Reasons and Divine Action: A Dilemma. In Kevin Timpe and Daniel Speak (eds.), *Free Will and Theism: Connections, Contingencies, and Concerns*. Oxford: Oxford University Press, 258–76.

Rissler, James (2006). Open Theism: Does God Risk or Hope? *Religious Studies* 42(1), 63–74.

Rissler, James (2017). Open Theism. In Matthew Braddock (ed.), *Internet Encyclopedia of Philosophy*. www.iep.utm.edu/o-theism/.

Salles, Ricardo (2012). Oikeiôsis in Epictetus. In Alejandro G. Vigo (ed.), *Oikeiôsis and the Natural Bases of Morality: From Classical Stoicism to Modern Philosophy*. New York: Georg Olms Verlag, 95–119.

Smilansky, Saul (2012). A Problem About the Morality of Some Common Forms of Prayer. *Ratio* 25(2), 207–15.

Smith, Nicholas D. and Yip, Andrew C. (2010). Partnership with God: A Partial Solution to the Problem of Petitionary Prayer. *Religious Studies* 46(3), 395–410.

Stump, Eleonore (1979). Petitionary Prayer. *American Philosophical Quarterly* 16(2), 81–91.

Talbott, Thomas (2009). God, Freedom, and Human Agency. *Faith and Philosophy* 26(4), 376–95.

Swinburne, Richard (1998). *Providence and the Problem of Evil*. Oxford: Oxford University Press.

Taliaferro, Charles (2007). Prayer. In Chad Meister and Paul Copan (eds.), *The Routledge Companion to Philosophy of Religion*. New York: Routledge, 617–25.

Thornton, Allison (under review). Petitionary Prayer: Wanting to Change the Mind of the Being Who Knows Best.

Timpe, Kevin (2005). Prayers for the Past. *Religious Studies* 41(3), 305–22.

Timpe, Kevin (2013). *Free Will in Philosophical Theology*. London: Continuum Press.

Timpe, Kevin and Speak, Daniel (2016). *Free Will and Theism: Connections, Contingencies, and Concerns*. Oxford: Oxford University Press.

Van Inwagen, Peter (1983). *An Essay on Free Will*. Oxford: Oxford University Press.

Van Inwagen, Peter (2006). *The Problem of Evil*. Oxford: Clarendon Press.

Veber, Michael (2007). Why Even a Believer Should Not Believe that God Answers Prayers. *Sophia* 46(2), 177–87.

Wahlberg, Mats (2020). Divine Revelation. In E. N. Zalta (ed.), *The Stanford Encyclopedia of Philosophy*. https://plato.stanford.edu/archives/fall2020/entries/divine-revelation/.

Watson, Gary (2003). *Free Will*. Oxford: Oxford University Press.

Weil, Simone (1959). *Waiting for God*. Translated by Emma Craufurd. London: Fontana Books.

Whitcomb, Dennis, Battaly, Heather, Baehr, Jason, and Howard-Snyder, Daniel (2017). Intellectual Humility: Owning Our Limitations. *Philosophy and Phenomenological Research* 94(3), 509–39.

White, Heath (2019). *Fate and Free Will: A Defense of Theological Determinism*. Notre Dame, IN: University of Notre Dame Press.

Wierenga, Edward (2002). The Freedom of God. *Faith and Philosophy* 19(4), 425–36.

Wolf, Susan (1990). *Freedom within Reason*. New York: Oxford University Press.

Zagzebski, Linda (2017). Foreknowledge and Free Will. In E. N. Zalta (ed.), *The Stanford Encyclopedia of Philosophy*. https://plato.stanford.edu/archives/sum2017/entries/free-will-foreknowledge.

Zimmerman, Michael J. (1985a). Sharing Responsibility. *American Philosophical Quarterly* 22, 115–22.

Zimmerman, Michael F. (1985b). Intervening Agents and Moral Responsibility. *Philosophical Quarterly* 35, 347–58.

Acknowledgments

Over the years, many people have helped me understand some of the main philosophical issues involving prayer and overcome some of my (many) mistakes in trying to think through them carefully. My earlier published work suffers from pessimism about petitionary prayer that I have been able to overcome (at least to some extent) thanks to conversations with these people. Special thanks are due to William Hasker, Daniel and Frances Howard-Snyder, Daniel Johnson, Scott Hill, Caleb Cohoe, and Sabrina Little for reading a complete draft of this manuscript and providing extremely helpful comments that led to significant and substantial improvements. I would also like to thank George Mavrodes, William L. Rowe, Thomas P. Flint, Eleonore Stump, Ronald L. Hall, Michael J. Murray, Alexander Pruss, Katherin Rogers, Meghan Page, Kate Finley, Michael Rea, Kevin Timpe, Isaac Choi, and Allison Thornton for many helpful conversations over the years concerning these issues. Two anonymous reviewers for Cambridge University Press also offered helpful comments and suggestions concerning an earlier draft of this manuscript. The errors that remain are my own, of course.

Cambridge Elements ≡

Philosophy of Religion

Yujin Nagasawa
University of Birmingham
Yujin Nagasawa is Professor of Philosophy and Co-director of the John Hick Centre for
Philosophy of Religion at the University of Birmingham. He is currently President of the
British Society for the Philosophy of Religion. He is a member of the Editorial Board of
Religious Studies, the *International Journal for Philosophy of Religion*, and *Philosophy
Compass*.

About the Series
This Cambridge Elements series provides concise and structured introductions to all the
central topics in the philosophy of religion. It offers balanced, comprehensive coverage
of multiple perspectives in the philosophy of religion. Contributors to the series are
cutting-edge researchers who approach central issues in the philosophy of religion. Each
provides a reliable resource for academic readers and develops new ideas and
arguments from a unique viewpoint.

Cambridge Elements ☰

Philosophy of Religion

Elements in the Series

The Problem of Evil
Michael Tooley

God and Emotion
R. T. Mullins

The Incarnation
Timothy J. Pawl

Ontological Arguments
Tyron Goldschmidt

Religious Language
Olli-Pekka Vainio

Deprovincializing Science and Religion
Gregory Dawes

Divine Hiddenness
Veronika Weidner

The Axiology of Theism
Klaas J. Kraay

Religious Experience
Amber L. Griffioen

Feminism, Religion and Practical Reason
Beverley Clack

Pantheism
Andrei A. Buckareff

God and Prayer
Scott A. Davison

A full series listing is available at: www.cambridge.org/EPREL

CPSIA information can be obtained
at www.ICGtesting.com
Printed in the USA
BVHW042024050422
633465BV00009B/105